CW00971881

Take A Peek . . .

Edited by Michelle Afford

forwardpress

First published in Great Britain in 2007 by:
Forward Press Ltd.
Remus House
Coltsfoot Drive
Peterborough
PE2 9JX
Telephone: 01733 898108
Website: www.forwardpress.co.uk

All Rights Reserved

© Copyright Contributors 2007

SB ISBN 978-1 84418 471 2

Foreword

'Take A Peek . . .' Turn the page . . . Step into another world. Everyone gets the bedtime blues so here's your chance to conquer them. Inside 'Take A Peek . . .' you can take the magical journey into your dreams.

A sparkling collection of poetry and prose makes this anthology the perfect way to take yourself off to bed. If you're looking for a rhyme to make you giggle or a story that takes you somewhere else then simply turn the pages and let the authors do the talking. Magic and mystery, beasts and bumps in the night as well as humour and heroics mean you'll never want to put it down!

'Take A Peek . . .' then jump right in!

Contents

The Poems

The Lawrencian Monkeys

(For the residents of The Lawrence School, Lovedale, Ooty, India)

The Lawrencian monkeys have the latest of hair styles
Oh yes! The Lawrencian monkeys are way too cool
The Lawrencian monkeys are intellectual guys
Though the sight of ripe bananas can make them drool

Their tails swinging from shingled roofs
These monkeys slide into classrooms full of scholars
Picking up pens by the handfuls as proofs
Of their talent for jobs requiring starched white collars

So woe to the boy or girl who perchance
Laughs at the monkeys' cerebral abilities
They might as well as be banished to France
Than face what could be the worst of calamities

For the Lawrencian monkeys won't tolerate
Clowns, buffoons, dullards and duffers
They follow strict laws on their simian estates
And act swiftly against all and sundry trespassers

Recycling is an art, these monkeys have mastered
They duck into the school bins with practised ease
Their limbs get busy and their faces get plastered
But they'll pose alright, if you come and say, 'Cheese!'

The school's large dining hall is another place where
These simian wardens of etiquette regularly patrol
Forget the students; even the teachers aren't ever spared
If they come out chomping on a half-eaten dinner roll

So the students of The Lawrence School, it is rumoured
In their quest to keep these monkeys always good humoured
Collect nearly all the buns that they get for their evening tea
And, offer them up to the apes with a respectful: 'Hail to Thee!'
The monkeys then descend with heart-warming panache and charm
They eat the buns and trash the cups; that's all.
                    The rest are unharmed.

Rumjhum Biswas

Scary Biscuits

On a dark, stormy Hallowe'en night
Two scary biscuits had a fright.
One was shaped like a vampire bat.
The other like a witch's hat.
Bat said, 'Let's trick or treat,
Visit every house on the street.'

From the bakery window they crept
While all the good biscuits slept.
But outside things weren't as they thought.
Perhaps their biscuit mixture was too short.
Bat said, pointing to the sky,
'Is that a witch's broom flying high?'

An ugly face made them shudder,
It was a mask made of rubber.
Was that sound a skeleton's rattling bones?
Bat changed his mind, saying, 'Let's go home?'
'What's that funny purring sound?'
Witch's hat said as they turned around.

Close by was a large black moggy,
A sight which turned our brave biccies soggy.
They both decided to run away,
Live to frighten another day.
That cat nearly caught our biscuit chums.
Those scary biscuits almost ended in crumbs.

David Moss

Frustration

One day while I was home alone
I watched my dog trying to bury a bone.
He tried and tried in a different place;
Without success - he began to pace!

Back and forth he tried and tried;
I felt so bad I almost cried!
'You'd better stop right now,' I said,
'When Mom gets home you won't be fed!'

I didn't have the heart to say
'Try again another day'.
I finally gave his tail a tug;
'You can't bury a bone in the living room rug!'

John E Rockwell

Henry The Mole

Henry the Mole
Was a shy old soul,
He lived with his wife
And his son named Cole.
He spent all autumn digging a hole
Until he made a tunnel under the ground to call 'home'.
So when the winter came
And it was chilly outside
His family would have somewhere to snuggle,
Somewhere cosy to hide.
So be careful where you step
In the fields where you play
As you may wake him from sleeping
During the day.
In the night-time he is often busy again,
Searching for a snack or two
To take to his den.
Be careful not to scare him
If you spot him during the day or night
As he may become frightened
And run out of sight!

Camille Miriam Metcalfe

Wake Up Donny

Donny the Dormouse was a shy little fellow and oh how he loved
to sleep.
Most of his friends had been awake for hours when out of his hole
he would peep.
One day he decided, 'If I go on like this then life will just pass me by,
So from this day on I won't sleep in - well at least I will give it a try.'
But late next evening when Sammy Squirrel came round Donny
wouldn't wake up from his rest,
And no matter how loudly Sammy called out his name Donny stayed
snuggled right down in his nest.
So through the autumn while Donny slept on Sammy had to gather
in nuts by himself
But with a lot of hard work after many long weeks he soon had
enough on the shelf.
Meanwhile little Donny was now wide awake, being disturbed by
his rumbling tum,
But when he looked in his storehouse for hazelnuts there wasn't
even one.
When he told Sammy Squirrel that he had no food, he hung his
head in shame,
He had nothing put by for the winter months and he only had
himself to blame.
Well Sammy wasn't one to say I told you so and was more than
happy to share,
He knew his friend was sorry, and besides, he had plenty to spare.
Now every evening Donny gets straight out of bed and is as busy
as he can be,
And to pay Sammy Squirrel for his kindness he invites him every
Saturday for tea.

Eileen Wilby

Terror In Rafters' Garden!

Jamie, a skinny, gawky lad with spiky hair and freckles that covered the whole of his face and Davie, who towered over him by at least a foot, were discussing what to do over the summer holidays with Shaun, who incidentally was the shortest of them all. In fact, although Shaun was short, it was Davie's height that made Shaun look much shorter! Davie's height gave him the nickname of Rafters, somehow derived from giraffe! Shaun's nickname was just Shorty. Jamie; because of his freckles had managed to acquire the name Freck.

Freck, Shorty and Rafters didn't hear George, with his squeaky trainers walk up close. He used to be their friend until he took Rafters' bike one afternoon and didn't return it. He supposedly lost it at the shops. Of course he refused to own up but Shorty, who'd happened to be going to Rafters' house at the time, saw him, or so he says. In fact George has always strenuously denied it but he was still deliberately excluded from their plans.

'I've got an idea,' announced Freck, proudly. It wasn't often he thought of a half decent idea. 'Let's go camping. I've a tent we could use.'

'Brilliant idea,' remarked Shorty. 'But do you think our mums would really let us?'

'Yes,' answered Freck. 'Especially if we camp in Rafters' back garden. Then they'll know where we are and your mother will know her little shortcake is safe.'

'Don't call me Shortcake,' stormed Shorty, getting agitated at being referred to, as Mummy's little darling.

'Stop bickering. Great idea but why my garden?' complained Rafters.

'It's simple, you've the biggest garden. It's like a blooming jungle out there. Great for camping,' said Freck, sniggering.

It was unanimous, on the first night of the holidays they would camp in Rafters' back garden, if Rafters could convince his mum. Freck knew this wouldn't be a problem because Rafters could wrap his mother around his little finger. It was this reason that Freck suggested Rafters garden, than the excuse he gave about the size, but of course he wasn't going to tell Rafters that!

George heard everything. 'Can I come too?' he asked, stepping closer.

'Huh, not unless you find my bike,' insisted Rafters.

Freck, Shorty and Rafters turned their heads and walked away while George stood there seething at the remark.

Forward Press - Take A Peek . . .

The first day of the holidays had arrived. Shorty collected some sleeping bags and took them round to Rafters' house, while Freck brought round his tent. Rafters' mum kindly supplied some biscuits for a midnight feast. She also painstakingly put the tent up which took most of the afternoon because the boys didn't have a clue what to do.

'Right now lads,' smiled Rafters' mum. 'Rafters has the key to the house should there be an emergency, and I mean a serious emergency, after all it was your decision to camp!'

Night was falling quicker than any of them had anticipated and it was soon getting too dark to see properly. They scrambled into the tent to lie the sleeping bags on their chosen spot for the night.

'Not enough room to swing a cat in here,' moaned Rafters, trying to put his sleeping bag on top of Freck's neatly placed sleeping bag.

'My head's going there,' groaned Freck. 'Move your sleeping bag off mine.'

'Ya, like where do I put mine then?' grumbled Rafters, now getting grumpy at the lack of space.

'Alright, keep your hair on, I will turn my sleeping bag round and sleep the other side of it,' groaned Freck.

'Hey, listen. Can you hear a noise?' whispered Shorty.

'Quick, do the tent zip up,' cried Freck, not happy with the idea of an intruder snooping around. The noise was beginning to freak him.

'I can still hear it,' whispered Shorty in a shaky voice. 'Can you?'

The noise suddenly stopped. Everyone went deadly quiet. An eerie feeling swept through the air like something more sinister was around the corner. They didn't have to wait long. The zip of the tent slowly crept down an inch, all eyes now transfixed on the zip, to see if it would move again. A piece of crinkled paper flew through the gap. The zip then closed quicker than anyone could blink. Rafters plunged forward, grabbed the paper and quickly shot back, in case the zip moved. He unwrapped the paper. It read in bold black ink, 'death is near'. Shorty and Freck quivered.

'What does it mean?' squeaked Shorty. 'This better not be your mother playing a joke on us, Rafters' fear gripped his already rigid body and he started to cry uncontrollably.

'Don't be daft, my mother wouldn't do this,' cried Rafters.

'I don't know about that, she must've a sense of humour; she gave birth to you, didn't she?' laughed Freck, nervously hoping it really was his mother!

'Look, it's not my mum,' stormed Rafters, indignantly. He was about to let rip with verbally abusive language when he noticed Shorty still crying. Rafters didn't like to see his mate cry. Slyly, he winked to

Freck, without Shorty noticing, then announced, 'I reckon it's my next-door neighbour. He's always having a laugh at my expense. Isn't that right Freck?'

Freck agreed but he knew Rafters' next-door neighbour was at least eighty and rarely left his armchair, still he didn't want to alarm Shorty.

Shorty managed a half-hearted smile when Rafters then mentioned food. His eyes lit up as the biscuits appeared before him. His smile turned into an enormous greedy grin.

'Let's have our biscuits and ignore the stupid neighbour. He'll get bored soon and leave us alone,' smiled Rafters.

They all tucked in. Shorty didn't wait to finish what was in his mouth before shovelling more biscuits in.

Rafters cunningly managed to deflect the conversation by cracking rude jokes, which made everyone laugh until Shorty stopped. He could hear a rustling sound coming from outside the tent. Freck could hear it too. 'Can you hear that rustling sound?' spluttered Freck, trying desperately hard not to freak out completely.

The tent began to shake violently and with such force Shorty screamed in utter terror.

'Lie down so you don't get hurt,' shouted Rafters, as he threw himself to the floor. The pounding got more vigorous with thundering blows almost collapsing the tent. Rips appeared with each shuddering blow. Rafters decided to crawl sneakily to the front of the tent.

'Don't go out, Rafters, or you will be killed,' screeched Freck. He now believed in evil monsters although he'd swore blind that they didn't exist before.

'No chance of that,' confirmed Rafters. 'We've been locked in, good and proper.'

'Oh no, this is a serious emergency and we can't even get out!' shrieked Freck.

More blows rained down on the tent, weakening it from its fixtures.

'We're going to die,' yelled Shorty. He let out an ear-piercing scream, almost forgetting to breathe, until Rafters violently shook him.

Suddenly just as fast as it had started the blows stopped.

'Stop screaming and open your eyes, Shorty,' shouted Freck.

Shorty finally stopped screaming. Everyone was quiet. Terror engulfed them as fear filled the air.

'Look, the zip is moving,' said Rafters. 'It was jammed before.'

Another piece of paper flew into the tent and the zip closed again. This time it read: 'Own up or the devil will get you'.

'What does it mean?' whispered Freck, nervously.

'Someone has a secret which the others don't know about,' remarked Rafters, picking up the note.

'How did you work that out?' asked Freck. 'And why should that bother anyone?'

'It's obvious that whatever is out there knows of a deep secret and they want a confession or they will kill them,' replied Rafters. 'Look if anyone has a secret then tell us now, or die.'

Freck looked puzzled. He couldn't understand the logic of it all. After all, why would anyone be bothered about a secret.

'It's not me, that's for sure,' announced Freck, immediately. 'Is it you Shorty?'

Shorty's lips trembled, not with fear but sorrow and tears filled his eyes.

'I have a confession,' he whispered softly. 'Will I die if I confess?'

'No,' said Rafters, 'only if you don't.'

Freck looked over at Rafters. He was very calm considering the circumstances. In fact he had been pretty calm throughout the whole ordeal. Things were not adding up in his head. Rafters could see that Freck's mind was working overtime so he quickly sat Shorty down.

'Own up before it is too late,' spluttered Rafters. 'No one will hate you and this thing might go away.'

The tears in Shorty's eyes turned into a long, narrow river running down his cheeks. He took one deep breath and started to speak. 'I ... I took your bike Rafters, not George. I lied and blamed George because I borrowed your bike and rode it to the shops but when I came out it was gone. I panicked then I saw George that morning at your house, and I decided to blame him. I knew you were out because I had knocked on your door to confess about your bike but as I left, George turned up and I saw my chance to get out of owning up. I blamed George. I'm really sorry.'

'It isn't me you need to say sorry to,' confessed Rafters. 'It is George.' Rafters opened the tent and called George in. Here, you can tell him, yourself,' remarked Rafters.

Freck was even more confused. 'What the heck is George doing here?' gasped Freck.

'It's simple really. George said to me he saw Shorty at the shops with my bike. He said he didn't want to get Shorty into trouble but he saw him take my bike. My neighbour saw George and confirmed he didn't leave my house with a bike, so I had to believe him. We both knew that Shorty wouldn't confess unless his life depended on it, so we hatched a plan last night to scare him into confessing. We couldn't tell you Freck, in case you accidentally gave the game away,' admitted Rafters.

'You knew all along it was George,' shrieked Freck, 'blooming clever, if you ask me. I don't know whether to be angry or just relieved I'm still alive! But why pretend it could have been your old neighbour?'

'Well, Shorty was getting too frightened so I had to defuse the situation in case he had a heart attack on me and I didn't get my confession,' joked Rafters, knowing that George was getting carried away with it all.

Shorty stood up and looked at George. 'I'm so sorry I blamed you for Rafters' bike. It seemed the easy way out,' he confessed. 'Now I feel worse than when I lost Rafters' bike in the first place and I felt pretty rotten then!' Shorty wiped the tears from his swollen red face and turned to walk away.

'Where are you going?' asked Rafters, puzzled.

'You don't want me around so I'm going home. I hope one day you'll forgive me,' sighed Shorty.

'Don't be daft,' smirked Rafters, 'George and I made a promise. If you confessed, we'd all be friends again, just like the good old days, as long as you promise not to lie to your mates again. Ain't that right George?'

'Yep, sure is,' smiled George. 'Anyway I reckon we got our own back freaking you out like that. I'd say we're even.'

Everyone laughed, even Shorty.

'C'mon,' said Freck. 'We've wasted enough time already. Let's get down to some serious camping. Pass the biscuits Shorty, that is, if you haven't eaten them all.'

Shorty passed the biscuits.

'Hey, what about a sleeping bag for George? You are going to stay aren't you?' asked Shorty.

'Don't worry, mine's just outside the tent,' announced George as he went to get his sleeping bag. It wasn't long before they were all laughing together, even though space was limited!

Diane Beamish

Our Trev

Our hamster Trevor's a wonderful pet,
He hardly ever bites the vet.
But he's got a problem -
A troublesome one.
For he loves to chew,
And I don't mean gum!

He chews electric cables,
We worry he'll get fried!
He chewed my dad's best slippers,
And made a nest inside.
He chewed our mum's eyeshadow,
It turned his whiskers blue.
Has nothing been invented,
That our Trevor will not chew?

Then one day Dad said, 'Drat and blast!
That chewing rodent's chewed his last.
He's chewed clean through my underpants!'
'Oh please,' we begged. 'Just one more chance!'

We promised Trevor would be good,
And found for him a block of wood.
Now Trevor's jaws could not be fitter.
He even makes his own cage litter!

Jackie Buckle

Labelled

I know a boy who dresses funny
But I wouldn't stop being his friend not even for money
People call him funny names
And don't include him in their little games
He is one of my bestest friends
Even though he's not in the trends.

Elliot Michael Wooton (11)

The Teacher Creature

Beware of the Teacher Creature
It's from a mysterious place
Its language so totally alien
It could be from outer space

Maybe from a far-away planet
Way past the Milky Way
Sent here to work in our children's schools
To make them all do as they say

It's no use you trying to tame them
They know each and every trick
Don't try to whisper your secrets
They can hear through walls one metre thick

They are able to see around corners
They can be in two places at once
Their roar can be louder than thunder
In order to get your response

So as I deliver this warning
One thing still remains to be said
The incredible Teacher Creature
Has eyes in the back of its head!

Kath Cooley

Kind Kitty And Cheeky Chick

Today's tale speaks of most unusual friends:
A ferocious feline, frightened of hens
And a fluffy small chick, in your hand to hold
Bold and courageous, though not a day old.

Old Mother Hen, numb from weeks of hatching
Thus addressed her two dozen hatchlings:
'Now that you're finally out of the eggs
The farmyard awaits, let's stretch our legs!'

The youngest and smallest and cutest of all
Victim of quarrelsome clumsy feet fall,
One would go south, the other one north,
His feathery weight they would not support.

Shedding bitter tears in the basket he sat
Thinking of green grass, grain and worms fat,
The two feet engaged in foolish dispute,
Him - incapable of making them mute.

That's when our cat to step in saw fit,
Asking politely: 'Can I give you a lift?'
The dispute got sorted on her velvet back,
What are the feet for and who wears the hat?

From that moment on they're together as one,
Black cat and chick - strangest of union
No fowl will dare bite Kitty's sensitive nose
Little chick keeps them in check with the hose.

From dawn until dusk they are scratching about,
At night they scare mice singing duets aloud
Then quench their thirst with pasteurised milk
And dream of next day's adventures in silk.

Anna Lengyel

Bravest Of All

After several days of talking and listening to the elders, the time for action had arrived. Our unlikely hero named 'Howls Like A Wolf' - a red Indian brave was waiting beside his magnificent horse, ready to mount his steed and leave the reservation.

His fellow Indians were all engaged in the process of saying goodbye to their squaws and offspring. All were eager for the battle to begin. Their intention was to fight to reclaim land, which had once belonged to their tribe. Land which they believed belonged to them and which they wanted to return to their people.

Discussions between the elders and their opponents regarding the disputed land resulted in stalemate. To the young Indians, a battle was inevitable to solve this problem.

Howls Like A Wolf, was excited about taking part in the forthcoming event but also apprehensive. The twenty-five-year-old was a provider of food not a warrior. He always wore a headband with two white feathers. This day he stood resolute, bare-chested but wearing a red coloured string around his neck. This was the first time he had ridden into battle.

The need to speak, to reassure his wife was difficult when he himself did not know what to expect. The last time his people had fought, Howls Like A Wolf was only twelve years of age. Then his job was to remain on the reservation and look after his mother and younger sisters, until the other braves returned. Of course, he had heard the stories - had listened as elders recounted heroic tales of his ancestors.

His father, Stalks Like A Wolf, died in a similar land dispute battle when he was two years old. Howls Like A Wolf, did not remember his father but he was told that, when required, his parent had been a good warrior.

In looks, father and son were alike with piercing dark blue eyes, a small face and jet-black flowing hair. Their temperaments proved they were gentle beings, renowned for being hard to anger. Both men were brilliant hunters, having the ability to sneak upon their quarry until almost within touching distance. They then released their spears giving the quarry little chance of escape.

Howls Like a Wolf once more told his wife, Maya, that everything would be alright, soon he would return to her and his small son. He told his plans regarding the little one. He said he would teach Soars Like A Bird to fish in the nearby river - show him how to throw his spear correctly to obtain food. Howls Like A Wolf said he would show his son how to run quickly and teach him the art of hunting big game.

But Maya continued to weep, while rocking her son to sleep in her arms. Her fears did not diminish with her husband's words. *Surely,* she thought to herself, *the tribe had enough land.* But this thought she would never say aloud. Maya was scared, only twenty-three she had been with Howls Like a Wolf for two years. She could not stop crying, afraid of being left on the reservation with just the oldest Indian men, women and children. *Who would defend them from attack?* she thought, when all the braves were away fighting. Maya cried because she did not know what conditions her husband would have to face or how long he would be away. Reluctantly, she let Howls Like A Wolf give her a kiss on the cheek, after stroking the head of his sleeping son. Then Maya abruptly turned and walked back to her tent, unable to watch her husband ride out of the reservation into the unknown.

Howls Like A Wolf did not feel her despair when the signal was given from the lead horseman to mount his charger. From disorganised chaos, two thousand Indians quickly found themselves in well spread out lines. It was still early morning and a low hazy mist hung about in the valley. But the sun was rising and heat was beginning to burn off the mist. Soon there would be clear visibility ahead.

To the left of him Howls Like A Wolf became aware of a drum beat beating ever louder and faster. With a yell the large gathering moved forward. Our hero found himself in the third row from the front. It was not long before his horse, following others in front was moving at a swift pace. In his left hand Howls Like A Wolf held his trusty spear - a gift from his mother when he reached maturity. She said it had once belonged to her own father. Howls Like A Wolf's grandfather would be proud knowing his grandson carried the spear. The reins he clutched firmly in his right hand. Like many Indians Howls Like A Wolf was an accomplished horse rider and chose to ride bareback.

The warriors did not have to ride far before reaching the disputed land. On the horizon plainly seen was the enemy camp. The soldiers inside had been sent to the area to stop Indians taking possession of the land. Hearing a rumour that the tribe was about to invade the area an extra two hundred soldiers had been sent to the camp. They had arrived with many rifles and much ammunition.

But because it was still early not every soldier was prepared for an imminent attack. The mist had almost vanished. In the morning light a lone soldier on lookout duty spotted a movement. When he looked again the mass was nearer. Definite figures could be seen.

Realising how near the enemy were he gave an urgent signal on his bugle. He told nearby soldiers Indians were approaching. They looked and, seeing the same, rushed to tell others. In seconds the whole camp was aware of the impending danger. Rapidly dressed soldiers took their rifles and headed to vantage points to keep the land under their control.

Howls Like A Wolf could spy the soldiers' camp in the distance. Nervous excitement coursed through his veins. His young bay horse galloped faster, its white mane blowing frantically. Howls Like A Wolf glanced either side of him, saw his fellow braves, cousins, uncles and brothers wearing the same intent look on their faces. They had all taken part in earlier battles, knew what to expect. He, a novice, felt slightly afraid of the unknown but adrenaline carried him forward. An image of Maya and his son came to mind but he quickly dismissed it as on he rode. Over long, uneven blades of grass and small shrubs he continued. Tighter he grabbed his faithful hunting spear. Ahead he plainly heard gunshots, shouts, then cries of pain echoing along the valley. More shots followed by more shouts. Howls Like A Wolf tried to shut out these sounds as he progressed over the land.

He was approaching a small hillock but was unaware of the two soldiers crouching low in a dip beside it. All around him noises. Indians were close enough to the enemy to throw spears. Soldiers emerging from tall grass were being wounded, sometimes killed. Weapons picked up by the Indians were being turned on the soldiers. Soon the floor of the valley was littered with dead bodies from both sides and injured horses. Unseated horses were trampling over the fallen men creating a chaotic scene.

At the hillock Howls Like A Wolf's horse caught its front hoof on an uneven piece of land and began to fall. Simultaneously, the two hidden soldiers with guns primed took aim and fired. One soldier hit the horse in the side, the other soldier shot Howls Like A Wolf through his heart. By the time the impact of the bullet sent our hero sideways off his dying horse, he was already dead. His trusty spear slid from his hand as he fell.

The battle raged on for many hours. By late afternoon, one hundred and fifty Indians and eighty-five soldiers had died. Many more people were injured, some seriously. But then a letter arrived by messenger which stated that the disputed land was to be returned unconditionally to the Indian tribe. The land would form a border of the main reservation. A bugle signal was given sounding the soldiers' retreat. The letter was nailed to a stake for all to see. Battle-weary soldiers headed back to camp.

After a victorious chant proclaiming the winning of the battle, the Indians began the journey back to their loved ones on the reservation. Bodies of injured braves were placed tenderly on horses and an able-bodied man sat behind steering the horses, steadily but slowly back to their home. Dead bodies were heaped onto flat-bottomed wooden carts which were pulled by two horses. These carts had been at the back when the Indians charged and a man waited with them until required. The bodies were going to be buried at the sacred burial ground at the edge of the reservation.

Eventually Howls Like A Wolf's lifeless body was placed onto a cart. His small but athletic body was covered in bruises and areas of broken skin, caused by loose horses constantly kicking him. His headband was missing but the red coloured string given to him by Maya was in place.

The squaws watched the braves returning to the reservation but the men's body language did not immediately convey the result of the battle. Maya with her son cradled in her arms, pushed herself forward, looking for her husband. She became anxious when the first survivors arrived but none seemed to know what had happened to Howls Like A Wolf. *Someone must have seen him,* thought Maya, scanning the horizon.

Only a few stragglers remained, followed by the arrival of the dreaded carts, which contained the bodies of many young men. The carts went straight to the burial site. A mass grave was quickly dug by those Indians with some strength.

Lucky squaws took their warriors to their tents where they dressed wounds, fed and embraced loved ones.

But an eerie wailing sound filled the reservation as more dead men were recognised by their waiting families. Finally Maya saw the sight she had been dreading. There was Howls Like A Wolf's body. He had a bullet hole on his chest, a look of pain on his face. His body was being lowered into the grave.

Maya quickly handed Soars Like A Bird to another squaw and ran forward. Reaching Howls Like A Wolf's body, she managed to free the string from around his neck. Only then did she weep. Her husband was a gentle caring man. He was definitely not a born fighter but he had taken part in the battle to improve the life of his family.

Maya overheard the excited braves talking about their victory and return of the land to the tribe. She knew that the reservation boundaries would encompass the spot where Howls Like A Wolf and his companions had died. Maya realised she would raise Soar Like A Bird alone. But she would never let her son forget that his father died a hero. Maya proudly thought to herself, *he was the bravest of all.*

S Mullinger

Sammy The Snail

Sammy the Snail with his shell on his back
glides round our garden leaving a shimmering track
which gleams in the sunlight all silvery bright.
To me it is truly a beautiful sight.

But my mother thinks Sammy Snail is bad.
When he chomps through her vegetables this makes her mad.
She likes her cabbage and lettuces whole.
She says Sam's eating habits are out of control.

But snails need to eat just like you and me;
they just love cabbage and lettuce for tea.
They nibble on carrots and strawberries too
whenever they want something different to chew.

My mother told me if I could succeed
in teaching Sammy to eat only weed
he could stay in our garden forever and ever.
But I couldn't do this for I'm not that clever.

Now she says that Sammy and I really have to say goodbye.
Although I tried not to, this made me cry -
till a brilliant idea popped into my head -
I'll put Sammy in neighbour's garden instead.

Iris Melville

Teddy Bear

Watching shadows on the nursery wall,
Some petite and pretty, some grotesque and tall,
Alone and frightened I would be,
    But Teddy Bear is here with me.
Though battle-scarred, I love him so,
    A button where his eye should go,
A tattered arm, one short leg,
    No braver soul than my old ted.

Together we share the good and bad,
    He's the best friend I ever had,
When I cry, he soaks my tears,
    Cuddled in bed he calms my fears,
Other toys and books galore
    Clutter up the nursery floor,
When I am hurt they do not care,
    Or love me like my Teddy Bear.

E M Rose

From Lad To Man

'Where is my little cat?' asked old lady anxiously,
'Where oh where can my lovely cat be?
He's not wandering nearby nor chasing bees buzzing me!'
'Maybe he's climbed a tree,' small boy said helpfully,
Both looked up each tree in avenue, without success, woefully,
Peered into front gardens, cat nowhere to be found,
'I am worried,' said old lady, 'normally he's around!
LC is so naughty!' she remarked to her new friend.
'If he goes on like this he'll drive me round the bend!'
'Elsie!' repeated the boy, 'sounds like a girl's name to me!'
'It is!' she agreed, laughingly, 'but it's the letter 'L' and letter 'C'
Stands for lucky cat! Which sounds the same, you see!
When a kitten he was run over by delivery van from Leith,
Being a clever cat he lay quite flat beneath!
After the van passed by he flattened his ears to his head,
Raced back into his garden, hid in high flower bed.
Received no injury my ginger tiger-striped pet,
Stayed in overnight to be checked by the vet!'
'Not a scratch?' asked the boy,
'Not a scratch!' she echoed, 'to my utter joy,
Learned his lesson, his road safety code's superb,
Now stops to look and listen at every kerb.'
The little boy asked, 'Is this your cat running towards us?'
'Indeed it is!' she exclaimed, 'he looks scared and needs a fuss.'
A neighbour shouted, 'I have just found your cat locked inside
                                                          my shed,
He must have run in when I returned my moped!'
Thanking the neighbour, old lady said, 'Come LC time for tea.
Young man, here's a tip for helping me.'
First money ever earned, he thrust out his chest and strode home
                                                          like a man!

Hilary Jill Robson

The Crocus

Under the earth, in its tiny bed
a dear little crocus lay down
its sweet head, when a sunbeam

tapped at the earth and said,
'Wake up master crocus, it is time
you were out of bed.'

'O dear,' sighed the crocus, 'I am so tired . . .'
'Hurry up,' said the sunbeam,
'or you will be late.'

And off he flew to awaken the
rest, said the dear little
crocus . . . 'I'll do my best.'

So he pushed and he pulled till
the earth gave way and up he came
to the light one day and he

looked so gay in his coat of
yellow, that the sunbeam called
him, a gay little fellow.

Anne Safe

Anna And Izzy The Pocket Pink Fairies

(Dedicated to my sweet cousins Anna, Laura and Isabel)

Pink wands, pink wings, pink skirts and pink ballet shoes,
Pink-skinned, that's the colour of my pocket pink fairies.
Izzy from one pocket, her hair is brown.
Anna from another with her blonde curly hair.
With pocket pink fairies you can never be down.
They're dancing in my flower patch
And swinging on the gate latch -
My pocket pink fairies are here to stay,
In the flower dew they do play.
Those cheeky little fairies have put it in my shoe,
From fast fairies' pockets, comes fairy dust and glitter blue.
Then singing with glee my fairies stop at last,
Then to my surprise they take hold of my little fingers -
Not my pocket pink fairies, they're not that strong
Yet they whisk me through candy clouds, and prove me wrong.
Over my garden, over the glen, over the treetops, with fairy might.
How long will we be? What will we see?
Let's hope this journey lasts all night.

On our journey we see cats, cows, dogs and sheep,
A church, cosy cottage and the dragon's lair,
Then we fly over lake, green, deep.
Those naughty fairies have a dare.
Not pink pocket fairies, they wouldn't do such a thing
Yet sure enough they drop me in!
Water up my nose, water in my eyes, even up my skirt,
Now I'm at the bottom swinging in the dirt.
Pocket Pink Fairies to the rescue,
Lifting me up from waters, to skies of blue,
Back to my garden with the flu.
Then to my shock Mother arrives and Father too,
Into my pockets must little fairies go.
Grown-ups don't believe in fairies, you know.

Kimberley Otter

Tangerine Dreams

Tangerine dreams full of ice cream
Trickling treacle honeybees
Triangular chocolate temptations
Soda pop that tickles tonsils
Bubbles that go straight up your nose
Make you sneeze and your eyes water
Then everyone giggles with glee
Row on row of rainbow-coloured jars
All glittering in the sunlight
Tooth-decaying sweet explosions
Chocolate-coated nuts and raisins
Marshmallows that melt in your mouth
Liquorice sticks that make you sick
Lollipops on sticks colour tongues
Blue, red, green, yellow and purple
Fat stripy sticks of seaside rock
With names that go all the way through
Candy bars wrapped in silver and gold
Mouths full of scrumptious chocolate
Big bright eyes, candyfloss, sticky hands
Tangerine dreams full of ice cream.

D M Walford

Flower Power

Once in a coppice
A long time ago
As the first crocuses
Started to show
A very strong wind
With vicious glee
Tore through the bush
And ripped up a tree
Then it laughed at the damage
That it had just done
Like an unruly child
Hurting for fun

But the flowers fought back
Determined to bloom
Refusing to bow down
And be killed off too soon;
With their roots unharmed
And new growth coming through
They covered the ground
With white, orange and blue
Swiftly followed by
Pinks, yellows and reds
As fresh plants joined them
Proudly nodding their heads.

The wind backed away
Unsure what to do
And the sun shone and smiled
At the glorious hue
The trees sank their roots
As far as they could
And extended their branches
To look like a thick wood
Then, when it was over
And their bravery shown
The crocuses lay down
To rest all alone.

Betty Nevell

The Story Of The Helpful Vegetables

Little Ben the Brussels sprout
Really didn't want to go out
Cos his very best friend, Colin the carrot
Was stolen one day by a very big parrot
Who flew right down and took Colin away
Just when he was going out to play.

Even though it was really bad weather
The vegetable village got together
And all the beans and cabbages and leeks
Kept searching for Colin for nearly two weeks!
They really wanted to find him again -
Perhaps he was hiding in the lane? . . .

The peas and parsnips searched as well
And the cauliflower carried a great big bell
To warn them if the parrot came back
Perhaps they could catch him in a very big sack!

Then one day they heard a cry,
It seemed to come from quite nearby . . .
And everyone cheered - they'd found Colin the carrot
He didn't get eaten by the parrot!

They laughed and sang
And started to shout
'Let's take Colin home
And tell Ben the sprout . . .'

Now always remember - whatever you do
That vegetables really are good for you . . .
They will help you to grow if you eat some each day
And you'll get very strong in a healthy way.

But always remember . . .
Watch out for that parrot
Don't forget what happened
To Colin the carrot.

Sheila Kohn

Sooty

A little black kitten called Sooty,
Sat underneath a tree;
'Oh gosh, I feel so lonely,
I could do with some company.

I'm tired of watching birds,
Of chasing after mice;
If I had a friend to play with,
That would be so nice.'

Then up came the young tabby cat,
Who'd just moved to the house next door;
'What are you miaowing on about,'
And he put out a tentative paw.

'I feel very lonely,' miaowed Sooty,
'So I am really sad,'
'I'll be your friend,' said the tabby,
'My name is Cat the Lad.'

'Oh thank you Cat,' said Sooty,
His tail stood up straight and unfurled.
'I know with you as my friend, I'll be,
The happiest puss in the world.'

So Sooty no longer sits under the tree,
Feeling alone and so sad;
He's got a chum to play with,
His good friend Cat the Lad.

Shirley Brooks

Leon The Lizard

My name is Leon, the great lizard.
I belong to an old wise wizard.
I am a lot like the chameleon,
who can change colour to match the room.
My species walked this very Earth,
a long, long time before your birth.
Some people think we are scary,
but there's really no need to be wary.
I love to eat spiders and flies.
The wizard likes lizard tail pies,
but that's OK with me.
I can grow new tails you see.
To exercise I climb the wall
and rarely ever slip or fall.
I use my toes to hold on tight,
when dining out at twilight.
I'll act all innocent and shy,
when a fly or spider passes by.
It doesn't even notice me there.
I know it may sound a little unfair.
But when hunger strikes, it's time to eat,
I devour my fly or spider treat.
For when I feast I grow bigger,
therefore so does my tail's figure . . .
. . . and I am Leon . . . the great lizard.
A tail supplier for the old, wise wizard.

Joanna Muscat

A-Hunting We Will Go

The master of foxhounds decided one day
That he would go out and stalk his prey.
He'd find out where those foxes hide
And Bess his hound would be his guide.

She'd sniff them out, she would not fail
And so they set off down the trail.
Into the woods and along the road
And on and on they both strode.

Now foxes can be very sly
And they saw them coming by and by
And they both ran scampering down the glen
Until they reached their secret den.

Once inside they shut the door
And they lay so quiet upon the floor.
They didn't hear someone behind
Until he said, 'Now here's a find.'

And right behind them, there he stood
The largest badger in the wood.
They both took fright and off they ran
Down the warren to find their gran.

They knew their parents were not at home
And they had been told not to roam.
They knew their gran was old and frail
And dare not venture down the trail.

What would they do if Granny died?
They'd have no place to run and hide.
Those hounds would sniff and find her scent
They knew that they would not relent.

But down the warren safe and sound
Out of the way of any hound.
They chattered excitedly to their gran
And told the story of dog and man.

The dog and man turned for home
They knew that they could not roam
Any further, for the light
Was changing day into night.

And so they all went to their beds
The dog and man lay down their heads.
Those foxes with their parents lay
And dreamt of an exciting day.

H J Palmer

The Sneezedombobbilydoobly

Lurking round your doorway, ready to step in
Is the Sneezedombobbilydoobly
With a wide and happy grin.

Your house is where he wants to be, to check that you're OK,
He makes it his own business to pop in every day.
Maybe you have seen him, perhaps he was too quick,
To hide behind an open door, his disappearing trick.

His nose is long and pointed and the brightest shade of red,
For today he has a nasty cold and needs to be in bed.
To be your friend is what he wants, and he is happy when you're there,
He's generous and cheerful, just like your teddy bear.

Lurking round the doorway, ready to peep in,
Is the Sneezedombobbilydoobly,
With one whisker on his chin.

He's very kind and gentle, a fluffy sort of thing,
Scared of his own shadow although it looks very much like him,
He doesn't mean you any harm, in fact he loves you so,
That every place you visit, he would like to go.

He looks after your possessions, when you go to school,
Checks anything that's broken and mends it as a rule.
So when you hang your coat up, behind your bedroom door,
Just say hello and welcome, and you'll make his day for sure.

He's lurking round your doorway, why not invite him in,
The Sneezdombobbilydoobly,
You won't regret a thing.

Lindsey Priest

Night Shadows

I go to bed and try to sleep,
Head under the covers I suddenly peep.
What can it be, is something there?
Shall I get up, do I dare?

The night is dark, the room is black,
How much longer till the light comes back?
What was that I saw, it's moving about,
My lips are stuck, I cannot shout.

Petrified and stiff, I start to count sheep,
Finally, under the duvet, I drop off to sleep.
Now I'm asleep, there's nothing to fear,
But as I wake up I silently cheer.

Glancing around, things look just the same,
Who was that last night? I know it came,
The morning's arrived, bringing the light,
Then I start to wonder, will it be back tonight?

Kathy Pengelly

The Bubble Family

This is a story about a bubble family who live on the bathroom shelf in the Johnson family bathroom. In the Johnson family, there is Mummy Johnson, Daddy Johnson and sisters, Evie who is five years old and younger Jamie-Lee who will be three years old next week. The Bubble family come alive particularly at bathtime and only little children can see them. They look like ordinary bubbles to big people but Evie and Jamie-Lee see them as living bubbles.

The first time that Evie and Jamie-Lee met the Bubble family, Mummy Johnson had run them a lovely warm bubble bath and both the girls splashed and played with the bubbles whilst Mummy did her housework. They loved bathtime. Mummy had given them plastic jugs and spoons and they scooped the bubbles into the jugs and stirred and poured and played their bathtime games for as long as they were allowed.

'Look Evie,' exclaimed Jamie-Lee. 'Look at my bubbles; I've got millions and millions in both hands!'

'You can't have millions and millions,' giggled Evie. 'You may have hundreds and hundreds but not millions and millions!' she giggled again. Evie always thought she knew better than Jamie-Lee because she was the eldest.

Jamie-Lee giggled too and she blew them across the bath to Evie. 'Catch,' she cried and Evie cupped her hands into the air to catch the bubbles that floated down towards her.

'Whee,' called out a little voice. 'Catch me!' it said.

Evie caught the bubbles as they landed over her head. 'Where did that voice come from?' asked Evie. 'Jamie-Lee, was that you speaking in a squeaky voice?' she accused.

'No, it wasn't me,' replied Jamie-Lee nervously and she pulled her eyebrows together as she usually did when she didn't quite understand something or when something was wrong.

'It's me,' squeaked the little voice. 'I'm here in your hands. Take a closer look.' And cupped in Evie's hands was a round soapy little bubble, but unlike the other bubbles, this bubble had soft hazel eyes, a little dot for a nose and a small round mouth and its round body was made up of many pretty colours.

'Oh,' cried Evie with amazement, as she looked closer at the round, soapy little bubble. 'Jamie-Lee look, this bubble is talking to me!' she squealed.

Both the girls could not believe their ears and they could not believe their eyes!

'Don't be afraid,' pleaded the little soapy bubble. 'Little children can see bubbles for what we really are. Big people don't believe things out of the ordinary and because they don't believe, they can't see us,' explained the round, soapy little bubble.

The girls looked at each other and then at the talking bubble. 'What's your name?' asked Jamie-Lee.

'My name is Rainbow Pippa Bubble,' replied the round soapy little bubble.

'Where do you come from?' they chorused.

'I live here in your bathroom with my mummy Bubble, Daddy Bubble and my brother Philip Bubble,' answered the round, soapy little bubble who went on to say, 'and we have lots of bubble friends living in your street. There's Robyn, she lives at Number 48 and Zach and Tia both live at Number 54. We have bubble friends everywhere.'

Evie realised that the other bubbles in her cupped hands were not the same as Rainbow Pippa Bubble. They looked like ordinary soapy bubbles because they didn't have faces. One by one each bubble burst with the sound of a *ping* until all that was left in Evie's hand was Rainbow Pippa Bubble. Evie thought aloud, you seem stronger than ordinary soapy bubbles. 'Are you stronger?' she asked.

'Yes,' replied Rainbow Pippa Bubble. 'We're very tough. We don't burst as easily as other bubbles, but we still have to be careful not to be too clumsy,' she explained.

Both Evie and Jamie-Lee were so excited. This was like a dream come true. They had always wished their dolls could come alive and talk to them. Now they had a real living bubble friend.

'Where's your family then?' asked Jamie-Lee. 'Can we meet them too?' she looked around the room wondering if she could see them.

'Mummy Bubble and Daddy Bubble and Brother Philip Bubble have all gone to Bubble Land. We have to go there every now and then to visit the Bubble Queen,' Rainbow Pippa Bubble explained.

'Why do you need to see the Bubble Queen?' asked Evie.

'We have to top up our oxygen and only Bubble Queen in Bubble Land can do that for us,' explained Rainbow Pippa Bubble. She continued, 'When you are thirsty, you have a drink and when you are hungry, you have something to eat,' she went on to explain. 'Well, Bubbles have to have oxygen to stay light and bubbly.' Then Rainbow Pippa Bubble sprung into the air from Evie's hand. 'Whee . . . eee . . . eee,' she sang.

'That looks fun,' the girls laughed.

Then all of a sudden they heard a cough, 'oofh,' and then another, 'oofh.'

'It's Mummy,' they both said in alarm.

Within a flash, Rainbow Pippa Bubble first bounced onto Evie's head and then she bounced onto Jamie-Lee's head. 'I've got to go quickly, bye for now,' she whispered. 'I promise I'll see you both very soon.'

Evie and Jamie-Lee looked up to see Rainbow Pippa Bubble but she was nowhere to be seen. Evie turned to Jamie-Lee and said, 'This is so special Jamie-Lee. We've our very own Bubble Family!'

Mummy Johnson came from the other side of the bathroom door. 'Come along girls, it's time to get ready for supper.'

'OK Mummy,' they both giggled with excitement.

The following Wednesday, it was Jamie-Lee's fourth birthday and Jamie-Lee and Evie were having fun in their paddling pool in the garden. Mummy had rubbed total block sun barrier cream on them because it was a very warm, sunny day.

Mummy came out to the garden carrying a box of bath toys. 'I thought you might like to play with your bath toys,' she said.

'Oh yes please, Mummy,' said Evie. 'Can we have our bubble bath too?' she asked

'I can't see why not,' Mummy replied and a couple of minutes later she returned with their bubble bath. 'Here you are then,' and she poured some bubble bath into the paddling pool and laughed out loud. 'It will be like having a bath but in your paddling pool,' she giggled.

'Thank you, Mummy,' they said and they shared the toys between them.

'Now, you must promise to keep your sunhats on,' Mummy warned.

'We promise,' they chorused and Mummy turned to go inside.

Evie and Jamie-Lee shook their hands in the water to make lots of bubbles that rose so high they could hardly see each other! They were having lots of fun and were laughing so much that at first they could not hear the soft voice of Rainbow Pippa Bubble.

'Happy birthday,' sang Rainbow Pippa Bubble. But the girls didn't hear her faint voice. She tried again, 'Happy birthday Jamie-Lee,' she said in her loudest voice.

The girls looked at each other and Evie said, 'Be quiet Jamie-Lee, I think I heard something.'

Rainbow Pippa Bubble sang out again, 'Happy birthday Jamie-Lee,' and Rainbow Pippa Bubble jumped as high as she could and landed on Jamie-Lee's head.

Then all of a sudden, they heard another voice, 'Happy birthday Jamie-Lee,' and another bubble jumped as high as it could and landed on Evie's head. 'My name's Philip Bubble,' said the bubble. 'I'm Rainbow Pippa Bubble's brother and I've heard all about you.' Philip Bubble was slightly larger than his sister and he had a bluish purple tinge and Rainbow Pippa Bubble was made up of many colours.

'Let's play,' said Rainbow Pippa Bubble and then Philip Bubble. The Bubbles were having great fun. Rainbow Pippa Bubble warned, 'Remember what I told you before, we're tough little bubbles but still handle us with care.'

'Yes we will,' they said.

A few moments later, Jamie-Lee threw Philip Bubble into the air at the same time Evie threw Rainbow Pippa Bubble into the air. The two bubbles collided. 'Ouch,' they both cried. The two bubbles fell into the water giggling but all of a sudden, Rainbow Pippa Bubble started to cough. She coughed so much that Philip Bubble seemed alarmed. 'Oh dear,' he said, 'I must get Rainbow Pippa Bubble to Bubble Land quickly.' He scooped Rainbow Pippa Bubble onto his head and added, 'I must be quick, Rainbow Pippa Bubble needs her oxygen topped up and only Bubble Queen can do that for her. Within a flash, the two Bubbles disappeared into the air.

'Oh dear, will Rainbow Pippa Bubble be OK?' asked Jamie-Lee, pulling her eyebrows together as she usually did.

'I don't know,' replied Evie rather worriedly. But before long, they heard a whoosh in the air and their two Bubble friends were back. Rainbow Pippa Bubble looked very well indeed. She was very light and bubbly. 'Hello Evie, hello Jamie-Lee,' she called. 'We're back to play but I think we'll have to go now because your mummy is coming down the path.'

'We're so glad you're OK,' said Jamie-Lee.

'Yes, I'm very light and bubbly now,' she laughed. 'Happy birthday, Jamie-Lee!' she added and within a flash both the bubble friends were gone.

'What a lovely birthday this has turned out to be,' said Jamie-Lee.

'Yes, you've had a lovely birthday surprise,' chanted Evie. 'Let's go in and have some of your birthday cake!'

Rita Bridgman

The Gwyer Of Glen MacDoo

Up in the Highlands, roaming around,
The Gwyer lives deep underground.
Strong as an ox, small as a cat,
Bright orange eyes, teeth of a rat.
The Gwyer of Glen MacDoo.

It darts across the glen at night.
The Gwyer has infrared sight!
Ears of an elephant, leaps like a flea,
It's far too quick for us to see.
The Gwyer of Glen MacDoo.

It can hear a sniff from miles away.
Comes out at night, sleeps in the day.
Claws of a bear, wings of a bat,
One leg is thin, the other is fat.
The Gwyer of Glen MacDoo.

It visits homes and raids the cupboards
And climbs the stairs to see what's upwards.
It makes all the bumps we hear at night,
Because it's fun to give folk a fright.
The Gwyer of Glen MacDoo.

So, if you hear it in your room,
Don't lie in dread or fear or gloom.
It hates to hear folk laugh and sing
So have a giggle, that's the thing
To scare . . .
The Gwyer of Glen MacDoo!

Suzanne Bennell

Little Brown Rabbit

'Oh dear, oh dear,' cried a little grey mole,
'A fairy has tumbled into my hole.
It's full of mud and crawling things
And she can't get out for she's hurt her wings,
Oh help her white rabbit, I know you are good
And they say you are strong.'

'Don't bother me,' the white rabbit said,
And he shut up his eyes and his ears grew red.
'It's full of mud and it's sure to stick,
Upon my fur so white and thick.'

But a little brown rabbit popped up from the gorse,
'I'm not very strong but I'll try of course.'
His little tail wagged as he wobbled in,
And the muddy water came up to his chin.
He caught the fairy tight by her hand
And helped her to get to Fairyland.

She kissed him first on his wet little nose,
His wet button paws and his wet little toes.
When the day dawned on the morning bright
That little brown rabbit was silvery white.

Pat Seddon

Willy The Wasp

I'm Willy the Wasp and I like to be boss
Of my own little gang of bruisers
I do as I please, live life of ease
And don't get caught up with the losers.

I was buzzing around 'tween nest and hunt
When something tasty caught my eye,
A kitchen window left wide open, so
I just popped in to have a spy.

The kitchen's warm, the oven's on
The toaster has a heat ascending.
And then I smell the heather honey,
I can't resist, it's so heart-rending.

So I gobble and gobble and gobble
And then, sugared up, I fall asleep
And when the footsteps come along
My buzz has gone, I can't make a peep!

I flutter and stretch to no avail,
Make an effort but all is lost.
I'm stuck! The honey's got my tail!
Maybe I should have swum in the sauce?

'What's this?' I ask, 'The hand of God?'
As, giving out a strangled cry
The excitement is too much, I faint
As I feel myself being lifted high.

Then I wake up and realise the mother rescued me
And I'm safely in the bushes beside the big oak tree.
Now that I'm getting better, I have just one thing to say
When next you find a wasp in honey -
      you can be sure it won't be me!

Sheila O'Hara

Song Of The Llama

You have to laugh don't you?

That snooty young camel just came waltzing by,
It was all I could do not to spit in her eye!
Her toffee-nosed attitude gives me the hump.
If I could get at her I'd give her a thump-ing!
For years now the children have loved and adored me
Their sticky small fingers have patted and pawed me -

And then, out of nowhere this madam appears,
With the ugliest face, and the silliest ears,
A miserable look and an ugly-toothed smile
And really bad breath that is hardly beguil-ing!
But springtime approaches and soon she'll be moulting
And then they will see she is truly revolting!
So there!

Grace Galton

The Crocodile And The Dentist

Did you ever see a crocodile
That shook with fear?
If you promise not to tell
I will whisper in your ear.
'He was afraid of the dentist,
Can you believe that?'
He sat in the chair
And trembled like a cat who had just seen a mouse.
Did you ever see a crocodile
Whose teeth did chat
When he opened up his mouth?
He wished he was a mat that the cat sat on.
Did you ever see a dentist
Who shook with fear?
Well I'll tell you now
With a crocodile so near
His hands did shake and his knees went queer.
So the crocodile and the dentist
Shook with fear,
They trembled like jelly and they ran like deer for the door!

Joy Grant

What A Chick-A-Do

Ten fluffy yellow chicks and mother hen
All safe in their smart wire pen.
Then a grunt was heard, it was Big Piggy with his great big nose,
He poked his big nose under the wire netting frame, and over it goes.

The chicks were so frightened they ran far and wide,
Some in the stinging nettles did hide.
Poor mother hen clucked and called her brood.
She asked the farm animals for help, but no one was in the mood.

Then along came Dilly Duck saying some are in the rut,
Deep in the old cart track down by the old hut.
Next Shep the sheepdog came and drove the chicks like sheep
Back in the farmyard for safety keep.

Anne Churchward

Stanley And The High Speed Bears

It all started with the snoring. A giant breath that blew in and out of the forest. 'Shh' … it said, 'I'm hibernating,' as it blew all the bats from the trees. The giant breath blew the squirrels too. It blew them from their branches and they landed with great thuds on the ground. As winter covered the earth with snow and the snoring grew deeper and stronger, the forest became full of angry squirrels. Something had to be done.

The squirrels huddled together in the darkness of the forest. They needed to make a decision. The only way to stop falling out of trees was to stop the giant breath. The only way to stop the giant breath was to stop the snoring. The only way to stop the snoring was to wake up all the hibernating bears. So that was exactly what the squirrels decided to do.

'I think we should play bagpipes,' said one squirrel.

'I think we should dance in clogs,' said another.

But it was Eric the squirrel who came up with the best idea. It was such a brilliant idea it made all the other squirrels smile at the same time.

The squirrels began to follow Eric's plan. They moved quickly, filling their pockets with potatoes and climbing into the trees. And when the last squirrel was in position, they all looked at Eric and waited for the signal to begin.

While the squirrels waited in the trees, a boy called Stanley was lying in his bed, in his room, in his house on the edge of the forest. Stanley was staring at a piece of paper he had found in the forest. This is what it said:

Things to do when I wake up

1) Get up
2) Rule a country
3) Dance around
4) Win a dancing competition
5) Run to the Arctic Pole
6) Win a running medal
7) Chase some seals
8) Sail back
9) Win a sailing competition
10) Eat berries
11) Eat fish
12) Go to bed

Stanley wanted to know who could possibly have written such a list. 'How could anyone do so many things in one day?' he asked himself. 'How could they do things so quickly?'

There was a reason Stanley wanted to know who wrote the list, a reason he wanted to know how to do things quickly. Stanley had one burning ambition. He wanted, more than anything in the world, to be a runner. And the next day, Stanley was going to run in the most important race of his life. The winner of the race would be the best runner in the school. The best runner in the school would race against the best runners from all the other schools. The best runner of all the schools would race against the best runners in the world. And the best runner of all the people in the world would win all the running medals and sit in the sun and eat ice cream all day.

Stanley thought about the list and how it seemed possible for some people to do things very quickly. He decided that if he could find out who wrote the list, and ask them how they could do so many things in one day, he might find a way of running faster. And if he could run faster, he might just stand a chance of winning the most important race of his life. Stanley crept out of bed.

Did they really do all those things in one day?

And opened the window.

Did they really run to the Arctic Pole?

Stanley looked at the dark forest that held all the answers.

Did they really win a running medal?

And climbed out into the night.

As Stanley slipped through the angry, snoring forest, his slippers crunched on snow and twigs, and trees touched his hair with their fingers. Rain was sleepwalking from the clouds, dusting all the animals with snow. But then suddenly, Stanley stopped walking. His arms hung at his waist. His eyes wouldn't blink. His mouth wouldn't close. His legs wouldn't run. Trees that had been hiding the light from the stars twisted in the wind. And Stanley saw everything. He was surrounded by sleeping bears. And squirrels in the trees with potatoes in their pockets.

But before Stanley could do anything, Eric sent a whisper through the tops of the trees.

'Now!' it said, and was swallowed up by the night sky.

The bears started to twitch. Confused and restless, they folded their paws around their heads. Their bodies started to turn and their eyes started to open. Stanley looked at his legs. He knew he should run, but his legs wouldn't move. He stood still, looking at the bears with their teeth and their paws and their green eyes. The bears scratched their heads with their claws, and looked at the small boy in pyjamas. They had just woken up. So it must be summer. But it was snowing. So it must be winter. They were still tired. So someone must have woken them up too early. This was very annoying. They had lots of things to do. But not now. Now was the time for sleeping and dreaming of fish. And storing up energy for when it was time to do everything in one go. Another high-speed summer.

The bears looked at Stanley. And Stanley looked at his legs. Maybe it was time to run after all. And Stanley probably would have run right then, when the bears looked at him with their angry green eyes, if it hadn't been for all the squirrels that fell out of the trees and landed with great thuds on the ground.

'It worked!' cried Eric. 'We woke the bears up!'

'Yes,' agreed the other squirrels, 'but they look angry.'

Eric looked at the bears. The squirrels were right. The bears did look very, very angry.

'Sorry,' said Eric weakly. 'Would you like some potatoes?'

'No,' growled the bears. 'Why did you wake us up?'

Eric explained how their snoring was so loud and so strong that it blew all the squirrels from the trees. 'But how did you wake us up?' asked the bears. 'We didn't hear anything.'

'We stared at you,' said Eric. 'We put potatoes in our pockets to weigh ourselves down so we wouldn't get blown out of the trees and then we sat in different branches. We stared at you from every height and every angle and it woke you up. Even though you couldn't see us, you could feel us looking at you, wishing you would wake up.'

The bears scowled at Eric. They weren't impressed.

'What about you?' they shouted, pointing at Stanley. 'Why are you in pyjamas?'

'I want to find out who wrote this list,' said Stanley, clutching the piece of paper in his hand. 'I want to know how to go really fast.'

The bears looked at one another and started to whisper. Slowly, a bear stood tall on two legs and walked towards Stanley.

'I wrote the list,' said the bear. 'We can do things quickly because we spend all winter sleeping and dreaming. When we wake up we are so full of energy and have so many ideas of things to do, we do them all in one high-speed summer.'

Stanley thought for a while. He couldn't sleep all winter. But his race was only 20 seconds long. He liked sprinting.

'Maybe if I sleep deeply for one night and dream of running,' he said, 'I'll go extra fast for 20 seconds the next day.'

'Well it works for us,' said the bear. 'Can I have my list back now?'

Stanley gave the bear his list and thought about sleeping and dreaming of running.

But Stanley knew there was still a problem. The bears were still awake. And if they went back to sleep, the squirrels would start staring and wake them up again. The bears looked angrily at the squirrels. The squirrels looked angrily at the bears. And Stanley looked up at the trees that stretched across the sky.

'You bears!' shouted Stanley as he was struck by a brilliant idea. 'Go back to sleep and start snoring!'

The squirrels groaned.

The bears closed their eyes and curled their paws around their heads. It didn't take long for the giant breath to start breathing in and out again. 'Shh' ... it said, 'I'm hibernating.'

'You squirrels!' said Stanley. 'Climb those trees, jump out of them and flap your arms really hard.'

The squirrels climbed the trees, they jumped in the air, they flapped their arms and they landed with great thuds on the ground. But Stanley made them practise. And practise. And practise until all the squirrels were riding the air, using the giant breath to carry them across the sky.

'Flying squirrels,' Stanley muttered to himself. 'Brilliant. Absolutely brilliant.'

Back in his bedroom, Stanley listened to the sound of the snoring forest. His eyes closed and he slept more deeply than he had ever slept before.

When Stanley woke up, his legs jumped out of bed before he had even opened his eyes. They took him out of his room and out of his house. They took him back into the forest. They took him past the trees and the snoring and the flying squirrels, who were still practising gliding through the air. They took him all the way to school and to the start of the race.

Stanley stood at the start of the race track, and stared as his opposition began to gather. He felt his stomach grow heavy as a teacher stepped forward to start the race.

Stanley closed his eyes. He thought about the bears dreaming in the forest. He thought of how they would wake up in the summer and do everything they had dreamt of doing. He thought of his own dreams. He thought about winning the race. He thought about losing the race. He thought about how as soon as he lifted his right foot he would be running in the most important race of his life.

And then Stanley heard a voice.

'On your marks,' it said.

Stanley opened his eyes.

'Get set.'
And lifted his right foot.
'Go!'
And began to run.
The sky was full of flashes of light as Stanley ran.
Eric was taking photographs for his album.
The flying squirrels smiled and posed mid-air for the camera.
'I'll take one of Stanley too,' said Eric. 'I knew he'd win.'

Many years later, Stanley is in his garden, stroking his beard and eating ice cream in the sun. He looks through his kitchen window at all the running medals he keeps by the sink. *I've run a long way in my life* he thinks. *Maybe round the whole world three times.*

Stanley wonders what the bears will be doing this summer. Some are probably in Brazil, he thinks, climbing the tallest tree in the world. Some are probably winning singing competitions. Some are probably just eating berries.

When Stanley lies in bed, he listens to his wife snoring. 'Shh,' she says softly, 'I'm sleeping.' Stanley falls asleep smiling, as his wife opens her eyes, confused by the strange feeling that someone has been staring at her.

And when Stanley wakes up, his dreams carry on. They make his legs tingle as they take him round the world one more time, faster than he has ever gone before.

Alice Fenner

A Cat And A Mouse Tale

The mouse on the wainscot fain scuttled along,
Humming himself a grandiloquent song.
Whilst, high on a tallboy, a silhouette stirred,
That opened an eye, and ebulliently purred,
It stretched its full torso, and nothing is heard -
Until a faint squeal and a bump.
A tomcat, as black as the shadowy land,
Hath plummeted down from his tenuous stand.
With his claws digging deep, was a screech and a scrape,
A splinter of wainscot - like peeling a grape,
And blood - from the back of his enemy's nape?
Apportioned a terrible thump.

He looked, and he looked for that succulent mouse,
Under the wainscot, and under the house,
His eyes were as coals of a fire as they burned,
The night was as day as he twisted and turned,
It gradually dawned - the fate that he'd earned -
He'd missed by a whiskery mile.
E'er while, by-the-by, with the guile of a pro,
The mouse sought sanctum of odours that grow.
A trove for the gourmet beheld in its sight,
Rich cheeses and sweetmeats of Christmas delight.
It chose a rare Cheddar and took a swift bite -
And died there, contented the while.

Derek Haskett-Jones

My A, B, Cs

A is for the ants, they run around all day.

B is for my bed, to sleep the night away.

C is for the cuddles, I give lots to my mum.

D is for my dog, he loves going for a run.

E is for exercise, it helps to keep me trim.

F is for five fish, let's see them swim.

G is for the grapes, they grow upon the vine.

H is for hanging the washing on the line.

I is for ice cream, it's cold and tastes real sweet.

J is for juice, helps cool me down a treat.

K is for the kite flying high in the sky.

L is for my leg, attached to this is my thigh.

M is for the monkeys, there are lots at the zoo.

N is for my nan, she always has lots to do.

O is for oranges, they grow on a tree.

P is for the park, a great place to be.

Q is for the Queen, wearing her golden crown.

R is for riding on a bus out of town.

S is for the sun shining bright all day long.

T is for 'Twinkle, Twinkle Little Star' my favourite song.

U is for up and under, it's a great game to play.

V is for the van, driving on the road today.

W is for walking around the allotment grounds.

X is for xylophone, it makes lots of sounds.

Y is for the yacht sailing on the sea.

Z is for the zebra, he's all stripy.

Annette Smith

Pollyanna's World! - A Strange Dream

Meet Pollyanna, a very curious little girl with a crazy imagination. Pollyanna lives with her perfectly normal family, Mum, Dad and her older brother Charlie. Charlie is always teasing her.

'You're a weirdo!' he said.

'No, I'm not,' Pollyanna answered angrily and stormed off to her bedroom.

Pollyanna was bored with the world, she liked to imagine what things would be like if they were different.

Her bedroom is very strange, she has lots of toys on the end of her bed, but they are all upside down, and she likes to sleep underneath her bed instead of on it. She likes to draw her curtains in the day and open them at night! Pollyanna is rather peculiar and Charlie isn't about to let her get away with it.

One day after school, Charlie crept into Pollyanna's room. He placed a picture on her bed that he had painted of her at school. It was awful, and he knew Pollyanna wouldn't like it one bit.

That day, Pollyanna came home from school and went straight up to her room. She noticed the painting straight away. Charlie was secretly hiding, just waiting for Pollyanna to start screaming. She took one look at the picture and smiled. 'What a great imagination Charlie's got, I'd better go and thank him,' she said to herself.

Charlie was furious. He popped out of his hiding place; his face was puffed up like a balloon.

'Oh thank you Charlie, that picture of me that you painted, it's great!' she said.

'You're an even bigger weirdo than I thought!' he shouted and stormed off in a huff.

'How very strange,' Pollyanna whispered to herself.

At dinner time, Mum, Dad, Charlie and Pollyanna had bangers and mash. Pollyanna took her straw out of her drink and started to suck the mash up through it.

'You're disgusting!' Charlie shouted.

'No I'm not!' cried Pollyanna and she ran off into the lounge.

Mum and Dad were cross with Pollyanna and Charlie.

'It's very rude to argue during dinner time!' Dad said.

'Sorry Dad,' Charlie answered very quietly.

Pollyanna turned on the TV, the programme was all about wildlife in Africa. Pollyanna started to think, and she started to use her imagination. She thought harder and harder and then her ideas turned into a dream. Suddenly, she was surrounded by animals and insects, only the strange thing was, the animals were as tiny as bugs and the insects were the size of elephants! Pollyanna was terrified! She ran to hide under the bush nearby. She watched as a giant army of ants crawled over her, the noise was deafening, their big black bodies shadowing over her, turning the day into night. 'Help me! Anybody!' Pollyanna cried. Just then, something started to tickle her feet, so Pollyanna ran out from beneath the bush. When she looked down, there on the floor stood a tiny herd of elephants. Pollyanna bent down and looked closely at them and smiled, 'How sweet,' she said gently, so not to frighten them away.

Buzzzzzzz! Suddenly an enormous bumblebee flew over her head, the size of a small car, it was really scary!

Pollyanna started to feel very worried. She ran to a nearby lake and tried to wake herself up by throwing water over her face, but nothing happened, just a few tiny crocodiles clipped onto her hair and wouldn't let go. She had to run from a giant spider, and escape from the claws of a giant beetle. 'Aahhhhhhhhhh!' Pollyanna screamed!

'Wake up you freak!'

Suddenly Pollyanna was woken up by her angry, bad-tempered brother, Charlie. Pollyanna looked at the TV, the news was on. Pollyanna heard the news reporter say, 'News just in, giant ants are taking over the world ...'

Pollyanna turned as white as a ghost! 'Mummy!' she wailed. Charlie looked very confused.

As Pollyanna began to panic more and more a soft voice said, 'Wake up.' It was Mum. Pollyanna looked like she had just seen a dinosaur!

'Oh Mum, they said on the news there were giant ants! We're all going to be eaten up,' she explained to Mum in a panic.

'Charlie and I have been right here all along,' said Mum.

Charlie looked at Pollyanna as if she were mad. Pollyanna did feel relieved that it was all a dream.

That evening when Pollyanna went to bed, she slept like a log and she dreamt a wonderfully normal dream ...

Anne-Marie Howard

Sid The Spider

Our friendly pet is a spider called Sid
Sometimes he climbs up from the grid
But our cat runs away in fear
And my mam jumps upon the chandelier

But I like Sid with his many legs so long
When he runs up the clock it goes ding-dong
He dances on tippy toes like Fred Astaire
And snatches at all the flies just for a dare

How Sid can dance and how he can prance
He learned all his dancing skills in the ballroom of romance
He shimmies up the walls and dances on the ceiling
Sid says in all his legs he's got lots of feeling

Now my mam has bought a long-handled duster
She says it's called a special cobweb buster
She's going to use it to chase Sid out
Then he'll have to live in our downspout

Me and my bruvver think Sid should get a fairer chance
So we're saving all our money to send him off to France
But my mam says she's got arachnophobia
And it would be better if Sid emigrated to Zenobia

Then one day when my dad walked in
He trod on poor Sid then put him in the bin!

Elizabeth Farrelly

Butch The Rabbit

The children received a present, a rabbit named Butch
He lived thro' the summer in the garden in a large wooden hutch
To them he was so handsome with his beautiful striking head and ears
When overheard my two girls said he was their baby,
                                    that's what I heard

Every day they gathered sweet dandelion leaves and carrots
                                    for his meals
They treated him like a lord, he has a snob, he was well heeled.
In the summertime he liked to be free to roam among the warm grass
This was not a wild rabbit, by his breeding he belonged
                                    to the upper class

Thro' the winter's weather they carried his hutch and put
                                    it in the garden shed
I was the one to walk thro' the snow to feed him and change
                                    his straw-like bed.
He just loved to be stroked then he would lay so quiet
                                    when you brushed his fur
With a smile upon lips I am sure his long whiskers will sweetly curl

This noble rabbit would like his meals fresh daily, he just loved to eat
When he was angry and in a bad temper this spoiled animal
                                    would stamp his feet
Thro' the years our pet rabbit grew old I still think about that sad day
Our majestic Butch I found in his wooden hutch, our rabbit
                                    passed away

Then the children said we will clean his hutch and put it up for sale
They often talk about him, they loved his white fur and his bushy tail
When we talked to them we go to pet shop, we felt they were still sad
Then they said in one voice we are grateful, they said no thanks
                                    Mum and Dad.

J F Grainger

The Dippyinnytinny

Granny's got a tin,
it's called a dippyinnytinny,
it stands on Granny's shelf
and there are flowers on the liddy,
I know there are all sorts in it
cos one day I took a peep,

and Granny says the fairies
fill it up when I'm asleep,

there are beadies, and there's buttons
and ribbons by the score,
some crayons, glue and pencils,
and lots, lots more.
There are lots of little coins,
and soldiers made of lead,

and Granny says the fairies fill it up
when I'm in bed,

when I stay at Granny's house,
it's always such a treat,
to play with dippyinnytinny
before I go to sleep.
And when I'm tucked up nicely
I take a little peep
and try to see the fairies
who fill it up when I'm asleep.

Jacqueline Claire Davies

Our Little Budgie Joey

He's a cocky little devil
As he hurtles round the room
His antics keep us all in fits
There is no time for gloom

He always shares our dinner
And enjoys a drop of tea
He's never heard of worries
Like those that come to you or me

Sometimes he can be naughty
And ornaments will fall
Even wallpaper is not too safe
He will tear it from the wall

But he is young so we'll forgive him
Because of all the joy he can bring
Because there is no finer sight
Than our Joey on the wing

Don Woods

But That's Life

I have a father, mother, sister, brother
That makes four
All of whom I adore
I have uncles, cousins, a nan and dadda
Let me ask you - who could want more?

I have a house with a garden
And lots more besides
I have a dog, a hamster
And a horse that takes me for rides

I have toys and sweets
And I go to school
I have friends and teachers
Who show me the rules

But when I'm older
I'll need a boy or a girl
To find true love and have
A daughter or boy

(But that's life!)

Christian O Schou

The Bear And Duck

There once lived in a house of stone
a big grumpy bear,
he would let out an echoing groan
if someone came knocking there.

Then one day there came a tap
on the big bear's door,
but the bear was having a nap
and he wanted a little bit more.

So up he got and strutted,
the door swung and creaked,
he looked everywhere and tutted
until a little yellow duck squeaked,

'What do you want my tiny fellow?'
'Just a room for the night please.'
'Well in you come, you seem rather mellow
but don't give my house any fleas.'

So in he came and they chatted
drinking tea then wine,
eating fish which was rather battered
getting on jokingly fine.

Off to bed until morning
the bear made some toast
then the duck came in yawning
shaking the paw of his hairy host

'I must now leave and make it home
to you I give my heart
you saved me from a pointless roam
I unwillingly have to part.'

'But don't you want some toast my friend
and some tea to warm the belly,
I have some gloves you can lend
sit down and we'll watch the telly.'

The bear looked sad to lose a friend
and wiped away an ounce of tear;
then admitted he could not pretend
and asked the duck to stay for a beer.'

'But thanks I have to go for sure
my family will be wondering:
thanks for opening your door
I now go before it starts thundering.'

So off he went down the winding path
with the bear in the window sighing
thinking of the duck that made him laugh
paws together, gently crying . . .

G Culshaw

Mollie's Friendly Spider

Horace the hairy spider
Lived in a corner of Mollie's room
When her mum came in and saw him
She hurried for the broom
'Please Mum,' cried Mollie in despair
'He's just a friendly chap
When I sit at my desk
He climbs upon my lap
He has a lovely cheery face
And feels safe up on my knee
I love this little spider
And I'm sure that he loves me.'

Daphne Fryer

My Little Frog

I like my frog, I don't lie
Seeing him jumping in the sky
Wouldn't you like a little peep?
See him jump, see him leap

Green and slimy, he loves the water
Reminds me of my very first snotter
He swims around the pond every day
I like him slimy, just that way

It's not easy being slimy and green
I think I should call up the Queen
The girls they scream and run away
How can my frog get out to play?

Of my little frog, I'm really fond
I caught him in the garden pond
He's not a snivelly girl that's true
But what's a slimy frog to do?

James Peace

The Magic Mouse

A long time ago in the land of Cornnon in a great big castle lived King Albert and his wife Queen Sophie, with their baby daughter Princess Victoria. The princess was a beautiful little girl with blonde curly hair and wonderful blue eyes. She was so good that the King and Queen decided to hold a big party on her first birthday. Everyone important was invited to the party. The King also invited the King and Queen of Devonia, the country next to theirs. Victoria's godmother said she had something very special for the little princess, and would bring it with her to the party.

On the day of Princess Victoria's party everyone was rushing around to get things ready. The decorations were up and in the great dining hall the long tables were all set for the banquet. King Albert looked handsome, and Queen Sophie looked beautiful. They both greeted their guests, and everyone sat down for the banquet. After they had all eaten everyone went into the throne room. The princess was carried in by her nanny and given to the Queen. King Albert stood up and gave a speech, and then gave everyone permission to come up and give the princess her presents. One by one the guests walked up and lay gifts at the feet of the princess. Next to come forward was Victoria's godmother. She went over to the princess and gave her a small crystal glass cage with a little door. Inside was a little wheel that turned around and a tiny bed in the corner, but there was nothing in it.

Victoria's godmother asked to hold her goddaughter, and was given permission by the King, not knowing she was really a wicked witch. She picked up the princess, and muttered some words, then said, 'You will never see your princess again.' Then in the crystal cage appeared a little white mouse.

The Queen was crying for her baby and the King ordered the guards to seize the witch. The guards grabbed the witch, as she was struggling the little white mouse bit the witch on her finger. There was a bright flash and the witch disappeared, dropping the crystal cage on the floor. It smashed into thousands of pieces and the mouse ran away.

'We must find the white mouse,' cried the King, but the mouse wasn't to be found. All the people that came to the party looked all night for the white mouse but no one could find it. In the morning they all decided to go home. The King ordered all the cats and dogs to be put outside the castle and no mousetraps were to be put down. A new cage was put down in the throne room with fresh food for the mouse, if it came back.

Forward Press - Take A Peek . . .

In the castle everyone was sad, the King and Queen would not go out. They had everything they needed brought in. The cook in the kitchen started to get very angry because the kitchen was being overrun with mice and she had no cats to get rid of them.

10 years went by and the castle was the same sad place. Down in the kitchen the cook had to get a boy in to catch all the mice and kill them, but he was told not to kill a white mouse if he caught one, as that would be Princess Victoria.

The boy went around the castle every day to pick up all the mice in the traps he had put down. He put them all in a sack one by one, then he would go outside the castle to kill them.

One day as the boy was collecting the mice, he picked up a little white one with beautiful blue eyes. He popped it in his pocket and ran down to his room in the cellar. Finding a large glass jar, made some holes in the lid put some straw in the jar, then popped the white mouse in very carefully. After he had cleaned up the kitchen every night he was allowed to eat some of the food that was left. He put some of the bread in his pocket and went to his room in the cellar. 'There you are little mouse,' he said, 'I'm afraid it's not much.' The boy curled up on a pile of straw and went to sleep. It was the middle of the night and the boy woke up to the sound of a little voice,

'Please let me out, I'm cold.' The boy could not believe his ears, the mouse was talking to him. 'Yes, I can talk, because I am Princess Victoria.' The boy took the mouse out of the jar and put it on a stool. They talked to each other all night. The princess told the boy that when she had bitten the witch all the witch's magic power had come to her but because the witch had already cast the spell she could not stop changing into a mouse. 'The only way I can change back is to be placed on my throne on my 18th birthday,' she said. 'I can cast a spell by flicking my tail,' said the princess. 'What would you like?'

The boy sat on his pile of straw and thought, 'I would like to have a bed to sleep on.'

The mouse waved her tail, gave it a flick and by magic the boy was sitting on a bed with a lovely soft mattress. 'Do you want anything else?'

'No thank you,' said the boy, and they curled up on the bed and went to sleep. The boy left the mouse in the cellar while he was at work by day, and at night they would talk and practice magic.

One day as the boy was working in the castle, the cook went into his cellar room and found it all very tidy with a bed and blankets to keep him warm. She asked the boy how he got all the nice things in his room. Thinking the cook would keep his secret he told her about the magic mouse. The cook listened and then told the boy to go to bed.

That night the cook crept into the cellar and started to search for the magic mouse. After a while she found it under the blanket. Scooping it up in her hands she went out to the kitchen. 'Well then little mouse,' said the cook, 'now you can use your magic for me.' The cook was not a nice person, and for years she made the mouse use her magic for her. The boy knew what the cook had done, but could not do anything about it. He would have to wait until the cook slipped up and left the mouse where he could help it get away.

One morning the cook sent the boy off to gather up all the mice in the traps. She told the boy she was going to be out all morning, and went off to the market. The boy thought he would try to get the mouse, as the cook would be gone a long time. So off he crept into the cook's room and looked under the bed. There was the little mouse in the cage he had put it in. He picked up the cage and went to the tower in the castle, somewhere the cook would not find the mouse. The mouse was so grateful and said to the boy, 'For saving me from that horrible cook, I'm going to cast a spell and make you a prince.' With one flick of her tail the boy turned into a handsome prince.

The day after was Princess Victoria's 18th birthday, but the King and Queen did not want to celebrate. They did not know that the boy in the cellar had found the white mouse, and been so kind to her, saving her from the cook.

The new prince arrived at the castle door, he knocked loudly and was shown in to the throne room. King Albert and Queen Sophie came into the room. 'If you have come to see Princess Victoria she isn't here,' said the King, 'she was turned into a mouse on her first birthday.'

The prince then took a little white mouse out of his pocket. 'Could this be the mouse you were looking for?' He then went over and put the mouse on the throne, she flicked her tail and in a flash she became a beautiful princess, with long blonde hair and wonderful blue eyes. The prince went to the King and said, 'I would like to ask for Victoria's hand in marriage.' The King and Queen said yes and the wedding would be held the following week.

The day of the wedding had come, and everyone was dressed in their best clothes. The prince was standing in front of the King and Queen waiting for Victoria. She came walking down the middle of the great hall, she was beautiful. She was wearing a long white gown, and silk slippers on her feet. After they were married Prince William and Princess Victoria lived happily ever after, in a new castle that was given them by the King and Queen.

Yvonne Peacock

The Enchanted Wood

The moon rode fair on the cool night air
As I set out for the wood
Where the night-birds fly, and creatures cry
And the elms have always stood
Like watchers high against the sky
Faint menace in each limb
So most men fear to come too near
When evening's light grows dim.
My mind is such I fear not much
Mere fancy least of all
But even I may sometimes shy
And feel my scalp to crawl
When a candle burns among the ferns
I summon all my lore
To keep tight rein upon my brain
A glow-worm, nothing more.

My subtle care had set each snare
Last evening 'ere the sun
Had shed its light, and yet tonight
Can nary find a one.
With knitted brow I ponder how
My traps have lifted been
Till standing there I 'came aware
Of a wild and eerie scene
A cart, knee high, came lurching by
With hay and grasses piled
And on the hay a body lay
A crumpled pixie child
Was this my sin, to lay the gin
Which crushed that form so slight
As he lightly played in the woodland glade
In the stillness of the night?

Across the glade to the yawning shade
Of the hawthorns in the hollow
The wheels squeaked round but never a sound
From the awesome band who follow.
The mourners all 'neath two feet tall
But they shed never a tear
For I saw the gleam of the moon's pale beam
In their eyes as they trailed the bier
There in the wood unmoving stood
As rooted as the trees
I heard the sound of a questing hound
Throb faintly on the breeze
And felt the flow of blood like snow
Creep through each curdled vein
For I heard the knell of a passing bell
And the moon was on the wane.

That body frail, so still and pale
Filled my soul with remorse
An oath I swore I never more
Would shoot, or trap, or course.
And as I swore I moved once more
So stumbling headed home
Beyond the track I looked not back
As I crossed the furrowed loam.
Over the stream in the final beam
Of the moon now failing fast
Sprawled through the door to the flag-stoned floor
A-tremble, safe at last.
Mark well that I shall ne'er draw nigh
That 'chanted wood again
For I feared the knell of the pixie bell,
When the moon was on the wane.

J C Fearnley

Jack The Giant Killer

Atlantic breeze whips up the sands
Around the skirts of Cornish lands

Where lives the Giant our tale relates,
A foul seed born of spleens and hates.

Cormoran the Giant is on the prowl
His face fixed in a cursing scowl.

Astride the bubbling Tamar stream
He stoops to drink it dry.

Atop the moor of Bodmin high
He scoops up sheep that bleat and scream

And back and forth in search of meats
He scours the Marazion streets

Until good people cower away.
The Giant's greed no hand can stay.

Blood-red the dipping, dripping sun,
Blood-red the tor and quay and field.

O what on earth is to be done?
O who will stop and make him yield?

Such was the anguish of the mayor
Addressing townsfolk in the square

Across the strand from the giant's rock
As the church tower struck 12 o'clock.

And there beneath the legs of men
A small boy planned his stratagem

To stop the Giant's anarchy,
Restoring peace and amity.

Off slipped this tricky Jack-the-lad
Quick home to where his father had

The tools the boy knew he would need
To end old Cormoran's fit of greed.

And in the early morning light
On gleaming sands resplendent white

Jack blew aloud the precious horn,
His from the hour that he was born.

The blast was heard in every town
From Sharpnose Point to Plymouth Sound.

It shook the Giant from his bed
And cracked the walls about his head.

It split his pipe and broke his pot.
Anger fixed him to the spot.

Again, the blast came as before
And ripped the hinges from the door.

In open view they spied each other,
Jack and the Giant, one another.

And crashed the feet of Cormoran
Toward the boy whose task was done.

And crashed the feet of Cormoran
Just ten feet short of Cornwall's son,

When all at once the sands gave way
And down fell Cormoran beneath the clay,
Who never more would see the day.

Andrew Nuttall

Grandad's Runner Beans

Grandad grows runner beans
He grows them in his garden.
He gets a bowl, and takes my hand
And then we go to find them.

Grandad grows runner beans
We pick them in his garden
Long, short, fat and thin
We really do adore them.

Grandad grows runner beans
We help him in his garden.
We tend the beans to help them grow
There's nothing else to beat them.

Kate Mann

Pinky And The Ghost

Pinky sat huddled up in a corner of the attic surrounded by old, broken furniture. She felt cold, hungry and a little afraid. Darkness was descending on the cold December afternoon and she fancied that she could see shadowy figures all round her. But she would not budge. Let the ghosts devour her! Better still, maybe a kind ghost would come along, and she could request it to take her to her mother. She had gone to Heaven, everyone said. Nobody in this house spoke about Pinky's father. She knew his name was taboo so she never asked anybody about him. Pinky would rather go to her mother in Heaven than stay here. Nobody loved her.

Pinky was angry and hurt. *Monima* (aunty) and *Mama* (uncle) had scolded her like never before. Monima had even twisted her ear. She said Pinky was always up to mischief and lying about things. So what if Pinky made up stories sometimes? One day Didu had made *narkel nadus (coconut sweets)* and put them in a jar. Pinky thought she'd taste one or two but she ended up finishing half of them. When Didu discovered that the jar was half empty there was quite a commotion.

'*It must have been Bhulu,*' Pinky volunteered.

'*Don't be absurd, dogs cannot open lids,*' Didu said.

Monima gave Pinky a suspicious look and said sternly, 'Pinky, green horns grow on the heads of children who tell lies.' Then Monima felt Pinky's head and said solemnly, 'I think there are already two little lumps on your head.'

Pinky was scared out of her wits. Why should horns appear only on children's heads? Why not on adults too?

Pinky knew they also lied sometimes. The other day Monima and Mama had gone to the movies. Pinky had seen the yellow tickets in Mama's hands. But when little Bablu cried and made a scene, demanding to be taken along, Monima told him, '*We are going to Doctor Uncle. Do you want to be taken there Bablu?*'

Bablu promptly ran inside and hid himself under the bed.

Today things really got bad. In the garden, there was a bushy tree of beautiful red flowers. This tree was very special to Pinky because her mother had planted it. Pinky was very possessive and protective about it. She caressed the tree and even talked to it whenever she could. Then she had discovered that the newly married bride next door had been plucking flowers from the tree. Pinky had complained to Didu and Monima but Monima said, '*Don't be mean, Pinky. It is only some flowers.*' So Pinky decided she'd do something about it herself.

This morning, Pinky had gone to the neighbours' house and knocked on the door. When the bride had opened the door, Pinky had said, *'Don't pluck flowers from our tree. You don't know my mama. He has said if he catches you plucking flowers again he will eat up those apple red cheeks of yours.'* To Pinky's satisfaction, the girl went red with terror and fled inside. Pinky returned relaxed and happy.

She was sitting in the garden when Monima had yelled, *'Pinky come inside, fast.'* Now what, Pinky wondered! She went in and saw Mama pacing up and down the room. Pinky had never seen him look so furious. *'What have you told the bride next door, you shameless little brat?'* he thundered.

Monima twisted Pinky's ear and said, *'You are a fool and a little devil. Hold your ears and stand with your face towards the wall, you naughty girl.'* Then Mama said that Pinky was a bad influence on Bablu and instructed Bablu not to talk to Pinky. This hurt Pinky more than anything else did.

Didu came to Pinky's rescue and said, *'Stop it now. Pinky is only a child. She did not know what she was doing.'*

'Ma, you just spoil her,' Monima grumbled and dragged away a reluctant, crying Bablu out of the room. Mama stormed out too.

Pinky had felt so upset and humiliated that she'd decided never to go down from the attic again. She clutched her mother's picture and waited for the ghosts to come and eat her up. She sat there for a long time and almost fell asleep. Then suddenly, she saw a shadow take shape in a corner of the room. It was a skinny figure with a round face and two huge round eyes. He had thin arms and legs and two green horns on his head. He was wearing red shorts. He gave Pinky a toothless smile.

'Who are you?' Pinky asked.

'I am Lambu the ghost.'

'Are you going to eat me up?'

'No, I am not hungry.'

'Then take me to my mother. She is in Heaven.'

'I can't do that. But why do you want to go?' Lambu asked.

'Because nobody loves me here.'

Lambu laughed and said, *'Don't worry, we ghosts like naughty children, and I'll cast a magic spell, so that everybody here will love you.'*

Then Lambu started to shrink and finally became invisible. Pinky felt something crawling up her leg. She bent close to have a look and what she saw made her scream. Monima, Mama, Didu, Bablu and Bhulu came in and stood staring down at her. She was a sight with cobwebs

Forward Press - Take A Peek . . .

on her curly head, dusty legs spread out, clutching the photograph, eyes tightly shut and screaming loudly. A huge spider was crawling up her leg. Bhulu leapt at it but it scurried away and disappeared under a chair. Didu picked up Pinky and held her close. Didu reproached Pinky mildly, *'Here you are. We have been looking for you everywhere, and your mama has been to every house in the neighbourhood. We were so worried. You really gave us a fright today.'*

At dinner Didu prepared Pinky's favourite dishes. Bablu wouldn't leave Pinky for a moment and he was allowed to sleep with her, with Bhulu at their feet. Once alone, Bablu whispered, *'Did Ma hurt you, Didi (sister)?'*

Pinky replied in the negative. *'Ma is bad. I don't love Ma, I love you.'* Bablu put his small arms round Pinky's neck and put his soft, warm lips on Pinky's cheek.

Pinky's little injured heart was flooded with love for her small cousin. So someone did love her, after all. *'I love you too, Bhai, (brother)'* Pinky said, finally feeling happy and loved.

Santwana Chatterjee

The Squirrel

I was walking home from school one day
When I saw a shifty squirrel
He swung through the trees like an acrobat
With a fancy twist and twirl
I stood in amazement watching him
Like a gymnast on a ring
His body danced through the swaying leaves
I could almost hear him sing
He took no notice of who passed by
He never once looked down
The wind began whistling a tune
While he acted like a circus clown
The sky was changing colour
How long I stood there - I don't know
I didn't think I'd ever again
See such a magical show
Then with a final party trick
He somersaulted through the air
Spinning like a ballerina
With such gracefulness and flare
He ran around the tree trunk
Gripping tightly to the bark
The street lights now shone brightly
He looked like a superstar in the dark
Then he quickly scurried down the tree
And disappeared out of sight
Scampering through the forest
What else will he do tonight?

Amy Owens

The Bubble

I'm a little bubble,
Started out as soap,
Someone blew some air in me,
And now there is hope.

My belly's getting rounder,
My sphere expanding,
I'm a natural phenomenon,
My presence commanding.

With the light just right,
I have rainbows in my eyes,
I'm reflecting every colour,
As I drift to the sky.

Children are chasing me,
They jump and wave their arms,
I am floating ever higher,
Escaping their harms.

I'm a marvel, a miracle,
A dazzling attraction,
Everyone is watching,
My squeaky clean refraction.

I like it, I'm loving it,
I hope it won't stop,
Oh look, a pointy pine branch
Uh-oh I gonna …

Tyler Snidow

Queen Pinky Pop

In the far away land of Toffetto
Lived the Queen Pinky Pop Chocoletto
She consumed many sweets
And her favourite treat
Was to guzzle, while viewing operetta.

She chewed every minute of the day
And was left with no teeth, for decay
Had set in and rotted
Her fat mouth, besotted
With a greed that would not go away.

Every day she grew fatter and fatter
But her attitude was 'does it matter'
Keep the candy man happy
He's a really nice chappy
And the money I pay fills his platter.

So she ordered each shop in the land
To make sweets and deliver by hand
Every greengrocer, baker
Fishmonger did make her
A sweet, each a different brand.

Her subjects grew hungry and cross
Having no decent food was a loss
They could buy no more fish
No red meat for their dish
Just truffles and pink candyfloss.

Well, the King of Good Heart soon heard
And stated, 'It's really absurd
Those poor helpless folk
It's gone past a joke
And a Queen getting fat, it's unheard.'

So he sat, tried to think of a way
To end this sad news of the day
Then he shouted, 'A tin
And a long silver pin
And I'll name it *Operation Soufflé!'*

He demanded his very best cook
To find a good recipe book
Make a soufflé and slide
This long pin inside
And send it by hook or by crook.

Very soon the deed was done
And delivered by the next morning sun
The Queen took one look
All excited she shook
Screaming out, 'Eating this will be fun!'

The Queen's young advisor, Sir Bonn
Said, 'My lords where has this gift come from?'
But the Queen intervened
'From an admirer you fiend
Now enough of your tattle, be gone.'

Every eye in the palace was staring
At the Queen, could she be
Quite so daring
To eat this delight? She felt pure dynamite
And declared, 'It's for me, not for sharing.'

She lifted it up to the sky
And said the soufflé, 'Bye bye.'
With a gnashing and a slurp
It went down with a burp
And a satisfied look in her eye.

Then, oh horrors, she began to deflate
And fly round the room at a rate
Everyone was spellbound
But did not make a sound
As the Queen screamed out, all irate.

She vanished in front of their eyes
From her top half then down to her thighs
All that's left was a pin
And a large red napkin
'She's popped!' said Sir Bonn with a sigh.

Sarah Morris

A Giant Called Gogmagog

Have you met the giant called Gogmagog
Every morning he goes out for a jog
He stops for a rest upon a log
And there is joined by his best friend the frog

Who comes along but a black and white dog
He has been walking through a stinky old bog
The dog, the frog and Gogmagog
All sitting together on the log

I'm sorry to say, you're a stinky old dog
I know I am, I've been in the bog
Could you sit further up, enquired the frog
But the smell didn't bother Gogmagog

Stop your croaking you silly old frog
He only smells because he's been in the bog
He is welcome to join us here on the log
What a kindly old giant is Gogmagog

**Elizabeth Ann Compton
(Assisted by Joe, aged 7)**

The Steadfast Soldier

As nightfall crept in, all of the children were in bed asleep. The stillness was so near to complete but for one factor, out of the darkness, without fear, came a toy soldier so stout, his chest standing out. From off the shelf up above he swung down and ducked, not from fear but from the sheer drop within which he engulfed.

At last he found himself upon the ground where he looked around the room from where he stood. There were others just like him made out of plastic, tin and wood, who were all gathering around. As the toy soldier drew near they all turned around and peered, as if to say 'who are you with a muscly figure, body so true, looking so tough and brave, ready to slave'? Whoever came across his path he was ready to kick ass. 'Yo there,' he called, 'my name is Ray and I can see right through you all, whatever you may say, whatever you may do, I am here to protect you.'

Everybody was pinned to the ground, amazed with the sound of protection renowned. With a cheer and a shout of, 'At last we are helped out in our struggle against the monster who lurks within our territory without a doubt.'

This is the beginning of the story. Ray had to pull together an army of men to fight against this monster who was lurking amongst them. All that was for him to consider was an army of wooden soldiers to make the enemy shiver. He drilled them with facts about the army's ways, not too relaxed in order to conquer all that was against them so tall.

Now the time had come to have some fun as the door creaked open wide, an enormous monster came inside. It had whiskers on its face with a body of fur and four legs underneath it with a tail that curved. The eyes peered so strongly as green as they were with a groan in deepness from within its purr. The scene was now set for combat to commence against all odds to show each other's strengths. The soldiers lined up with Ray at the front, all yelling out loud to make it sound like a crowd. As they all charged forward with their rifles in the air, the creatures leapt forward and tossed the soldiers over the chairs.

When the battle had died down and there was only Ray left on the ground, facing the enemy with his head standing tall. 'I can tell you this,' waving his fist, 'you will not defeat me as I am Ray and can see right through you come what may.' Ray then threw his rifle to one side and as the monster chased it Ray shot to his backside grabbing his tail. The monster began to wail spinning around, trying to make Ray fall to the ground. But Ray would not let go, with one hand firmly grasped, he was ready to show who was the boss at last.

As the monster slowed down Ray grabbed a horn with one hand and let go with the other to the ground, he then made a bellowing sound. The monster leapt in the air with its fur standing up with despair. There was a mad dash for the door and he was seen no more.

Everyone cheered as the monster disappeared, gathering around throwing the steadfast soldier up above the ground up and down. A hero he was to them for evermore, that soldier Ray who stood so tall.

Work was done and it was time to move on. He said to his friends with an air of delight, 'There are others who need my help in this life.' As he waved farewell saying his last goodbyes, as I told you then and I am telling you now, I can see right through the author's eyes.

K Thompson

Camping

Slugs in the washing up are not nice
When frying fish on a camp stove, Dad adds spice!

Life may not be easy but it can be fun
Collecting water for washing up, under the sun.

We like the life very much, for a week
But then for more comfort, we sometimes seek.

Mostly it is Mum and Dad who get a little creaky
But after camping for a week, the children too are sleepy!

So, home we go until next year
And with the end of summer all shed a tear.

Barbara Tozer

Hidden in Your Garden

'Neath the brambly thicket
where sunlight dapples and plays
Mrs Mouse and her family
while away their days.
Gathering the honeysuckle buds
to lay around the door,
wild rose and jasmine
to carpet the dusty floor.
Wild mint and harebell
dry on the window sill,
foxglove, daisy, hyacinth
and yellow daffodils.
Grandpa Mouse sits quietly
rocking in his bluebell chair.
Baby Mouse plays at his feet,
Mother cleaning her hair.
The mice live here happily
in a home of warmth and care,
love and peace so bountiful -
there's always some to share.

Sheleen Hems

The Lonely Lemon

In the little egg tray, just inside the door of the fridge, sat the lonely lemon. Bought in haste one pancake day it had subsequently failed to be used due to a train delay and a headache.

Months went by and the lemon sat and watched as visitors to the fridge brought with them new arrivals or removed and used so-called favourites such as milk, cheese and English mustard.

Lemon had a friend for a very brief time at the beginning, Green Pesto. However, during a vigorous pasta renaissance in the following spring, Green Pesto had once again had its day, resulting in its final hour as an integral component of a delicious spaghetti, boiled egg and pesto afternoon snack.

Lemon was now alone, utterly alone. It had infrequently shared the egg tray with a piece of chocolate, but these had been such fleeting visits, a full-blown relationship, let alone a casual acquaintance had been impossible.

As far as Lemon could remember, no egg, not even for the briefest of moments had sat with it in the unit constructed purely for this purpose. This added to Lemon's feeling of rejection and the utter futility of existence.

Time had been cruel to Lemon, once vibrant and full of zest it was now a shadow of its former self, a dried up husk waiting for the mercy of a fridge-wide clean out … A clean out that never seemed to come.

Herge Smith

The Adventures Of Amazing Angie B

In the magical town of Lostie Angie B slept in her tree house peacefully. She woke with a crash of thunder that made her fall out of her tree.

The town of Lostie was sent into darkness and the townsfolk started to cry. The frown clowns were appearing everywhere. They had kicked a hole in the sky. The frown clowns' army got to work and in less than a day, they used their powerful vacuums and sucked all the colour away.

The frown clowns sat triumphant in their grey misery, but Lostie was no ordinary place, and neither was Angie B. She went to the highest mountains, and released a stream of sparkle kisses.

The frown clowns had one weakness, they could steal colour, but they could not steal dreams and wishes.

Sparkle kisses swept all over the place, washing the grey out of town, whilst Angie B flew across the fields, planting flowers in the ground.

The townsfolk started to fill with colour again as the fields burst into life and Angie B turned the clowns' frowns upside down by smiling and being nice.

The clowns now live in Lostie, but their frowns have gone away. They now blow bubbles of sunshine to help brighten people's day.

Richard Higgins

At The Bottom Of The Garden

I'd been fixing my fences in my garden, when I thought I saw an elf,
At first I thought I was seeing things, he crept in there by stealth,
This advice I freely give,
Although you might not understand what I am saying. This is where
we live,
We have lived here for centuries and no human has ever seen,
We are supposed to keep out of sight, by orders of our Queen.
She is a very rare beauty who rules with a very firm hand
We are all her subjects. This you must understand.
Of course we have our enemies. Too numerous to say.
That's why we carry a sword. When they attack, we try to slay.
Some of our number have died because of age,
Our Royal Queen is very sad, while we are full of rage,
Help us to build a barricade, to stop them attacking here.
Of course we are all so tiny, which fills us with fear.
But make no mistake about it, we will defend our homes to the end.
We wear tunics of green you know and within the grass we blend.
You are the first human privileged to see an elf, I thought I was
camouflaged so that I could not be seen,
In my tunic and my breeches which are made up like grass so green.
You must swear to keep our secret. Or we will have to disappear
for good,
We will have to build our Fairy Kingdom, deep within a wood.

James Ayrey

The Thoughts Of A Child

Last night I stepped into my room,
Scary thoughts stepped into my head,
Creatures lurking behind the door,
Monsters under my bed.

Thingies in my cupboard,
Wotsits in my drawer,
How on earth will I get to my bed though
If I'm too scared to step on the floor?

If I go in and somebody grabs me
Will I be able to shout?
What happens then if nobody hears me?
Would I or could I get out?

I thought about this and decided,
To take a run and a jump into bed,
To get nice and warm, and safe from harm,
With the covers pulled over my head.

Yvette Matthews

Daisy, The Monster And The SAS

Daisy's such a naughty child,
up to mischief all the time,
if she's not eating Mother's cakes,
she's drinking Father's wine.

So off to Grandma's she being sent,
they'll put Daisy in her place,
but no one saw the wicked smile,
across young Daisy's face.

She started off good as gold,
and quietly read a book,
then outside in the garden,
came across a little duck.

With both hands, Daisy picked it up,
and placed it in the sink,
took a tin of grandad's paint,
and painted it bright pink.

She hid the duck, in the fridge,
behind lettuce and meat pies,
that would give her gran or grandad,
a nice little surprise.

So when Grandad, peered into the fridge,
for a midday snack,
he thought he saw and heard,
a little pink duck go *quack, quack!*

He shut the door, with shaking hands,
feeling giddy and quite weak,
stumbled to his comfy chair,
and promptly fell asleep.

While Daisy's grandad soundly slept,
she removed his new false teeth,
and on the upstairs toilet seat,
she placed them underneath.

When Grandma Val sat on the loo,
she got such a nasty fright,
as Grandad's set of gnashers,
into her behind, did bite.

She screamed out loud, quickly stood up,
not knowing what to do,
'Something's bit me, call the police,
and it's living in the loo.'

So Grandad, phoned the police and army,
who sent the SAS,
after learning of his wife's dilemma,
and her great distress.

They abseiled down the outside walls,
put a sniper on the roof,
and when they stormed the bathroom,
their vests were waterproof.

But no fearless monster could they find,
living in the loo,
as to where it went, the soldiers,
really didn't have a clue.

All they saw was Grandma Val,
with a smile, so wide and bright,
looking like she'd grown
a new set of teeth overnight.

They packed up their ropes, put on their coats,
and the SAS went home,
leaving Grandma, in the bathroom,
with her smile, stood all alone.

When she'd found out it was Grandad's teeth,
that gripped her fleshy rear,
she'd thought, *how on earth have these false teeth
made their way in here?*

Then Grandad, had shouted up the stairs,
'Don't worry, here's the army,'
and Grandma Val thought *oh my gosh,
they'll all think I've gone barmy.*

So she'd popped the teeth into her mouth,
which had formed a ghastly smile,
in Gran's mouth, there were more teeth,
than a full-grown crocodile.

Daisy, ran up to her gran, crying and upset,
while she laughed inside,
and thought, that was the best prank,
she'd pulled yet.

But when she looked up into Grandma's face,
Daisy began to scream,
Grandma was now a toothy monster,
from a horrid dream.

Grandma saw Daisy's fear,
and thought, *now here's my chance,*
revenge for all those times,
she's led me a merry dance.

'I'm the creature from the black lagoon,
living in the loo,
and I want Daisy for my dinner,
on a lovely barbecue.'

As Daisy fled through the door,
back to Mum and Dad,
Grandma said to Grandad,
'Let's hope that stops her being bad.'

Grandad got his false teeth back,
and they closed the bathroom door,
while from deep inside the toilet,
out reached a long arm … and a claw.

Christopher Taylor

Hamish Has A Job

'Hello Hamish,' said Jean. Jean is the person Hamish lives with. Hamish is a very large cat, almost a small tiger, golden brown fur, with black stripes, and a very long and bushy tail.

Jean was surprised when she opened the front door and Hamish wasn't on the car roof. This morning Hamish's nose had been pressed up to the door and when Jean opened the door Hamish had run up the stairs.

He ran into the bedrooms going into each wardrobe as quickly as he could, when he was satisfied nothing was upstairs he came down looking in the hall cupboard, then into the living room, he looked behind all the furniture and in all the corners, there was nothing there.

Looking from side to side Hamish walked into the kitchen, he was good at opening cupboard doors, even though he was not allowed. He knew that he would get shouted at if Jean saw him. He had no choice this time, he had to go into the cupboard, there was nothing there and Jean hadn't noticed him as he went from cupboard to cupboard. He walked passed the freezer, as he passed he looked underneath it, there crouching in the corner at the back of the freezer was a mouse, although Jean was washing the dishes he could not tell her, so he sat down and waited for a long time. At last the mouse ran from behind the freezer and Hamish chased it round the kitchen and round Jean's feet just as Jean carried a pan of cold water across the room. *Crash* went the pan onto the kitchen floor; splash went the water all over the floor, *bump* went Jean onto her bottom in the middle of the water.

The mouse was so frightened that he ran out of the open back door with Hamish close behind him, for once it wasn't Hamish's bottom that got wet.

Hamish was proud to have chased the mouse out of the house and for the rest of the day he walked with his nose and his tail in the air.

Graham McNicol

The Girl Who Wished On A Star

One frightful night when the sky was dark,
the thunder was roaring,
and the dogs did bark,
a small girl called Lucy watched the hard rain pouring.
She wished the storm would stop,
for the dogs to be silent,
for the rain to stop pouring and for the sun to show up.
So come morning time when the sky was quiet,
Lucy looked outside and to her delight,
all that was left were clouds and a sky so bright!
She looked even closer and saw there was a smile,
the clouds were looking down on her at least for a while.

Sarah Peacock

A Poem From Grandad Geoffrey

On Sunday we all went to Kew
Mummy and Daddy, Sophie too
And Uncle Marc and old Grandad
(Although he's old, he's not too bad)

We saw the pumps all made of steel
And shining copper tubes as well
And great big machines which made a noise
And a little place where there were toys

Then there was a train and we went for a ride
With wooden seats; we sat inside
A little door made very sure
We couldn't fall out on the floor

At first the train just made a hum
Until at last a steam one did come
And it whistled and puffed and panted so loud
It almost deafened the watching crowd

We came back to the station and the engine stopped
So we alighted - (new word; it means we got off)
And we went back to the museum and then, what joy!
Daddy bought me an engine, well, really a toy

So we all had a lovely family time
And this is the record of it all - in rhyme!

Geoffrey Speechly

The Snoggleford's Nose

The snoggleford was troubled
and knew not what to do,
for as he passed the sorcerer's house
a wayward spell broke through.

It landed on his shiny nose
and gave him such a shock,
for with a flash of purple light,
his nose became a rock.

From that day, he did not snore,
nor could he smell the cheese,
but when he caught a winter cold,
he found he could not sneeze.

This surely was a problem,
he went to see the nurse
who gave him horrid medicine,
which made the problem worse.

He went back to the sorcerer
who simply laughed and said,
'At least your nose is nice and blue
and not a sickly red!'

But when he saw the great big tears
upon the snoggleford's cheek,
he waved his wand and told him,
'You'll be better in a week.'

The snoggleford went home again,
and cheered aloud next day,
his nose was back to normal
for the rock had gone away.

Jillian Henderson-Long

A Christmas Tale

A streak of fire lit up the sky across a misty horizon and whilst Mr Morris was in the garden collecting firewood, his wife was decorating the Christmas tree, ready for when their two children returned from school. The tree looked really festive and shone and glittered with tinsel and pretty fairy lights and after standing on a chair, Mrs Morris added the finishing touch by putting a fairy on the top of the tree.

Afterwards, Mrs Morris set about wrapping the children's Christmas presents. There was a cowboy and Indian set for their son, and a Barbie doll for their daughter. *I hope that the children will enjoy the presents that Santa has bought for them* she thought, and to her surprise the fairy at the top of the tree answered her by saying, 'Yes, but what games are they going to play?'

Mrs Morris was astonished and looked at the fairy.

'Why it's simple, the cowboy and the Indian will compete for the love of Barbie of course!' Mrs Morris exclaimed and the fairy laughed.

'You think that Barbie could really love a cowboy or an Indian? I don't think so. Santa should have got Barbie's friend Ken!' The fairy retorted.

Mrs Morris was cross at this and argued, 'Of course Barbie could fall in love with a cowboy or an Indian!'

The fairy then said, 'Well, I'm going to prove you wrong!' With that she waved her magic wand. The toys stirred in their boxes and after several muffled shouts and groans, they tore their way out of their boxes!

Mrs Morris was surprised and said to the fairy, 'Now what have you done? These presents have to be wrapped and put away before the children get home!'

The 30cm high cowboy and Indian were soon walking around the living room, stalking each other and talking about who was the strongest and who was the fittest as Barbie stirred from her sleep before also climbing out of her box!

The Indian was astounded by Barbie's beauty, although she was not what he had expected as a squaw for his wife. The cowboy thought that she looked strange in glittery pink trousers and a blue disco top! Soon the Indian was boasting to Barbie about how she could be married to the chief of the Apache tribe, as he was, and the cowboy was saying how she could be head cowgirl of his ranch and own many fine horses.

Mrs Morris watched in amazement as this happened, before Barbie finally replied, 'No, my heart belongs to another, that of Ken!'

Forward Press - Take A Peek . . .

The cowboy and the Indian were both annoyed by this and so the Apache Indian spoke of the valleys and the trees where they could roam, hoping to inspire Barbie. Barbie was not impressed, and neither was the cowboy, in fact he became so angry and jealous that he began to shoot at the Indian with his gun! The Apache retaliated by firing at the cowboy with his bows and arrows! Barbie became frightened by this and hid behind the Christmas tree.

Soon afterwards there was much noise as the cowboy and the Indian began to chase one another, with the Indian howling and the cowboy whooping at the Indian and trying to catch the Indian with his lassoo!

'May the best man win then!' Shouted the cowboy.

The Indian defiantly replied, 'I will have this woman as my squaw!'

They both then began to search for Barbie, who in desperation had begun to climb up the Christmas tree. Soon all three of them were climbing the tree, with Barbie ahead, and the cowboy and the Indian in fast pursuit.

'Help! Help!' The Barbie cried out.

Mrs Morris shouted to the fairy, 'Do something!'

The fairy waved her wand but nothing happened. 'I can't!' She cried helplessly. 'The magic spell to change them back won't work!'

Shortly afterwards, the Christmas decorations on the tree were being pulled down as the cowboy and the Indian chased and fought with one another. 'Plink!' Went the Christmas baubles as they fell down to the ground followed by more tinsel.

'That's enough! I've had enough!' Mrs Morris shouted just as Barbie reached the top of the tree. 'You're a bad fairy, you shouldn't have cast that spell!' Then she climbed back onto the chair and reached for Barbie, to bring her back to safety.

The fairy watched too and said, 'I'm sorry! I'm sorry! I know, I can cast another spell.

Pine needles, pine needles fall to the floor,
Cover them
From their knees to their shins
To stop their wicked grins.

Pine needles, pine needles fall to the floor,
Cover them
From their hands to their arms,
For them losing their charms
And trying to cause harm.'

The fairy then waved her wand and watched as the cowboy and the Indian fell down onto the carpet. The pine needles fell from the tree too, but as soon as they hit the air, they whirled around tiny bits of tinsel and then soon sewed the cowboy and the Indian into the carpet, rending them both hopeless and helpless.

'What are we going to do now?' Mrs Morris asked the fairy. The fairy replied that she would try the magic spell again, and she waved her wand. Finally the toys became still and Mrs Morris climbed off the chair, relieved. 'Now, that's enough sky-larking for you!' She snapped at the fairy.

The fairy was sad, for she had only wanted to prove that she was right. 'I know, I'll make you happier by helping you to put the Christmas decorations back up!'

'No,' Mrs Morris said firmly, 'I've had enough of you and your antics!'

The fairy wouldn't relent though, and kept on pleading as Mrs Morris wrapped the toys back up. 'Alright then,' Mrs Morris said at last. 'What do you propose to do?'

'Your china doves on the mantelpiece, I need to borrow them.' The fairy said. Mrs Morris sighed and finally consented.

The doves then came to life and started to fly around the Christmas tree, putting all the decorations back onto the tree. Shortly afterwards the tree looked beautiful again. Mrs Morris was amazed and thanked the fairy.

The fairy then waved her wand again, and said excitedly, 'One last task!'

'What's that?' Mrs Morris asked, surprised. At that moment the doves flew out of the window! 'Oh no, what have you done?' Mrs Morris asked the fairy. 'They'll never come back now!' She said dismayed.

'Trust me,' said the fairy and she suggested that Mrs Morris swept up the tinsel.

'I'll never trust you again!' Mrs Morris replied crossly and went and fetched the broom. When she returned, she found that the doves were cooing around the lights with some tinsel and some mistletoe!

'Good luck to you with your romance anyway Mrs Morris,' the fairy exclaimed. The doves returned to the mantelpiece and Mr Morris entered the living room.

'Why, you've done a wonderful job, well done, mmm let's kiss under the mistletoe,' he said and they did.

Mrs Morris then put the toys away for Santa to collect and the children gasped in awe when they returned from school and saw the Christmas tree.

'Wow, who did this?' The children asked in unison.

'Oh Mommy and Santa's little helpers,' Mrs Morris replied with a warm smile.

Colette Breeze

The Mushroom Men

The mushroom men in the garden grow
Big and small, as white as snow.
Basking in the morning sun,
They lie happily with other vegetables having fun.

Baby mushrooms play hide-and-seek
Whilst the elder mushrooms bathe or sleep.
Middle-aged mushrooms wait to be cooked
When garden keepers get out their kitchen books.

'Who will be next?' they quietly say
As the back door opens and children come out to play,
Behind come the bigger men with spades
To dig them up, these helpless yummy little prey.

'Run for your lives,' the mushrooms say,
As the big monster kneels and digs away.
They run with the breeze with all their might,
But sadly the mushrooms' pleas blow away with the gushing
                    of the trees like day turns into night.

And up they're plucked to the basket they go,
Away from the cool garden, indoors alone,
Come inside my tasty friends,
The bacon is cooking and the bread is fresh,
I've got some salt to sweeten you up.

All I can do is wish you luck,
I'll just get a pan so wait patiently on my worktop here,
While I turn up the heat on my steaming fire.

But off they go when his back is turned,
Back through the kitchen where they were brought,
Their little legs running like a caterpillar's walk
To the garden to where they lay,
Saved for today
But people like their vegetables,
Fresh mushrooms are a tasty thought.

'Where did all the mushrooms go?
I brought them in I know,
Did I imagine today?'
He picks up his bowl to collect them again,
But low and behold it begins to rain.

'Never mind,' he says, 'no mushrooms on my plate again,
Yet tomorrow is a warmer day
So I'll go out and pick those tasty veg till none remain,
For next year more will surely grow again.

Bryony Freeman

Didn't Mean It

Yasmin the fairy sat on the edge of the new baby's crib. Yasmin had come to make a good luck wish for the dark-haired little baby girl and she knew she had to word the wish very carefully for it to come true, so with her elbows resting on her knees, her chin resting in her hands, she studied the baby, thinking deeply. After ten minutes Yasmin knew she had found the special wish. Sprinkling fairy dust upon the baby girl's head, Yasmin, pleased with herself, was just going to give the new baby a kiss on the cheek, as the wish passed from her to the baby, (because the wish wouldn't work if it wasn't sealed with a kiss) when a Sprog landed on the baby's pillow. Yasmin was horrified. The brown-coated Sprog had seen Yasmin fly through the baby's bedroom window and had followed her. Realising Yasmin was one of the golden-haired fairies with the delicate pink and blue costume who visited the new babies, the Sprog knew what she was going to do and he wanted that wish for himself. If he could catch the wish before Yasmin kissed the baby, the wish would be his.

Yasmin held onto the wish desperately, fluttering around the baby's head, trying to avoid the Sprog and give the baby a kiss, but the Sprog was too quick for her and she flew until she couldn't fly anymore because her wings were tired. Yasmin landed on the top of the set of baby drawers next to the baby's crib for a rest.

The yellow-haired Sprog grinned up at Yasmin, as he pranced around the baby's head, his big black boots where the brown and green tunics which the young Sprogs wore, kept all of their ideas and wishes, making dents in the pillow.

Yasmin rested for a while until she felt she was able to try flying again. Her job must be completed before she could go back to fairyland, but the Sprog was determined to have the wish for himself, shooting in-between the baby and her trying to catch the wish as it left Yasmin and before the wish reached the infant, but Yasmin kept tight hold of the wish, trying to find the right moment before she let it go. No matter how hard Yasmin tried, the Sprog seemed to be there before her. This contest went on all night, even after the baby had been fed and changed and was again asleep.

Morning came, which Yasmin was very pleased about as by now she was quite exhausted and as the wishes could only be delivered at night-time when the baby was asleep, she knew she would be able to rest in the daytime. Finding a comfortable spot at the bottom of the baby's crib, Yasmin laid her weary body down and went to sleep.

The Sprog stretched out on the baby's pillow, knowing by doing so he would be the first to know when the baby girl was put to bed. He cat-napped all day. Sprogs didn't need as much sleep as fairies so they had an advantage over them and as sometimes the fairies had to travel a long way from Fairyland to where they were going they needed their rest. Yasmin awoke with a start. The baby girl's mum was placing the baby in her crib which had woken Yasmin up. *I must have slept all day,* thought Yasmin, *it's a night-time already,* and she stretched her delicate little body.

The Sprog glowered, he had been having a wonderful dream where he had all of the fairy wishes in the world in his boots, when he was rudely awoken when the baby's pillow was suddenly removed from under him and he fell off. Just as suddenly the pillow was returned to the same spot landing on top of the Sprog, flattening his yellow spiked hair. The Sprog crawled out from under the pillow hoping that the fairy hadn't seen what had happened, but Yasmin had and her peals of laughter rang in his ears.

Luckily adults can't see sprogs or fairies, unless of course they want to be seen.

The contest continued, but Yasmin had no luck that night either. When it got to the fourth night and Yasmin hadn't complete her mission, she knew she had to do something and quick, her wish was becoming heavier to carry around with each passing night, so she sat down and thought what to do. On the fifth night Yasmin said to the Sprog, 'How would you like to have some extra special wishes?'

The Sprog's ears waggled, changing into different shapes as they did. Yasmin knew she had the Sprog's attention by what was happening with his ears.

'Do you see that long-necked green bottle on the window sill?' said Yasmin to the Sprog, 'I placed some extra special wishes for you in there.'

The greedy Sprog could hardly contain himself, but he knew if he left the sleeping infant he would lose the wish Yasmin had for the child.

'I know what,' said the Sprog, 'will you promise to come with me until I have had a look in the bottle and see the wishes for myself.'

'But of course,' said Yasmin. 'Come, I will even show you one,' and flew over to the round, bobble-bottomed bottle and took one of the special wishes out. The Sprog landed on the window sill and tried to grab the special wish off Yasmin, but Yasmin quickly flew to the top of the bottle, dropping the wish inside. The garden Sprog climbed up the bottle, putting his hand into the bottleneck trying to catch the wish, but it had gone down to the bottom of the bottle where it rested with the other special wishes, glowing softly. The Sprog was furious.

'They are yours,' said Yasmin, 'if you still want them, but I don't think your boots will go down the neck of the bottle. I will stand guard over them to make sure none of your other wishes and ideas escape if you leave them here with me.'

The Sprog looked suspiciously at Yasmin, but his greed got the better of him. 'You really mean all of those wishes are for me?'

'Yes,' said Yasmin, and with that the Sprog took off his boots, tied the laces around the neck of the bottle and dove headfirst into the bottle. Grabbing hold of all the special wishes the Sprog tried to climb out of the bottle, but the inside of the green bottle was smooth and he couldn't. Yasmin grinned at him, then emptied everything in the Sprog's magic boots into the bottle. The Sprog couldn't move. Yasmin quickly found the stopper for the bottle and placed it very firmly in the top. Yasmin kept hold of the magic boots though, because she knew if he did manage to get out of the bottle he would be able to keep all of the ideas and wishes in there.

Thankfully Yasmin went and completed her wish, kissing the baby gently on the cheek, then, she flew through the bedroom window taking the Sprog's magic boots with her back to Fairyland. Yasmin would tell the Master of Sprog Land about the Sprog and where to find him, knowing it would be a long time before he acquired another pair of boots.

The Sprog Master sent the black carriage pulled by the worker bees for the Sprog. The hornet pulled the stopper out of the green bottle, letting all of the wishes and ideas escape, bringing the brown-coated Sprog with them, who landed unceremoniously on the window sill, standing guard with his sting at the ready to ensure the Sprog entered the carriage.

The Sprog Master told the young Sprog the losing of the boots and the utterly selfish reason they had been used for, personal gain were the two worst sins a Sprog could commit, he would be banished for a year and have to live with the slimy sharp-toothed Dags under the broken flower pots beside the potting shed. *And if that doesn't teach him* thought the Sprog Master, *being nipped by the Dags for a year, nothing will.* The Sprog Master watched the young Sprog as he was taken away for his punishment. The young Sprog shouted over his shoulder as he went, 'I didn't mean it.'

The Sprog Master sighed, he hated being so hard on the young brown-coated Sprog, but there had to be some sort of retribution. *If he didn't mean it, why did he do it, it's just that some Sprogs had to learn the hard way,* he thought, *that is if they want to learn and learn by their mistakes.*

All of the young brown-coated Sprogs coveted the orange coats worn by the elder Sprogs and the earned respect they got, it's just that it takes some Sprogs a little longer than others to get them, unless of course a Sprog enjoyed spending a year every now and again with the sharp-toothed Dags.

Reana Beauly

Florence The Bunny With Only One Sticky-Up Ear

When she was born, it soon became clear,
That Florence had only one sticky-up ear.
The other fell flat away from her head,
And no matter what her mother frequently said,
She knew she was different, not like the others,
And often got teased by her sisters and brothers.

So then she started to sleep through the day,
Constantly frightened of what others might say.
She ventured out alone in the night,
Nibbling carrots and cabbage in the silver moonlight.
Her night-time feast only disturbed,
By the sun rising and the songs of the birds.

So much time in the dark and her eyes grew stronger,
And she could see fields that stretched on for longer.
Not rolling in the dirt, her coat became whiter,
And in the moonlight it shone brighter and brighter.
Then one night she grew quite tense,
Something was moving in the field by the fence.

It silently crept nearer and nearer,
Its outline now getting clearer and clearer.
Florence could make out a fox lurking up ahead,
But in the summer the bunnies were using the field as a bed.
Instead of being safe in burrows way down deep,
Here they were, out in the open, fast asleep.

She woke them all up, one by one,
Pointed to the burrows and whispered, 'Run! Run!'
And her fluffy white coat, clean and bright
Led them all to safety on this frightening night.

And Florence with her one ear up and one ear down
Soon became the talk of that bunny town.
The tale of the fox, down by the fence
And of the bunny with super sixth sense.
How Florence had bravely stayed and not run
And saved the fluffy tails of everyone.

Jo Brooman

Keep The Planet Healthy

Listen! Can you hear the message that's echoing around the world
Of the fight to save the planet and the costly lessons learned?
The Earth is dying we are warned, overheating and pollution.
The greenhouse effect and acid rain, the ozone layer and global pain.
Thousands starve while food mountains grow,
The Third World needs wheat and grain.
Giant tankers spill their oil and pollute the world's seas and oceans.
Giant problems for the world's leaders to solve with the United Nations.
But what of the issues closer to home, just what is to be seen?
Of our contribution to keep the planet healthy what has this been?
Lead-free petrol is an encouraging sign, less air pollution,
Recycling of paper, glass and cans is helpful to the solution.
Sprays, asbestos and lead-based paints are being banned at last.
Conservation of woodlands and wildlife helps to protect our past.
Greenpeace and the Friends of the Earth and others wage the fight
To keep the planet healthy for our children which is their own birthright.

Terry Daley

The Great Explorer

I really like polar bears,
Polar bears are neat,
I love them from their polar ears,
To their great big polar feet.

I love the way they go sliding,
Down mountains on their belly,
I know they do, I've seen them,
On Planet Earth on the telly.

Mum says when I'm older,
Maybe twenty-two or twenty-four,
I can go to where they live,
With my backpack and explore.

I'll have to take a friend with me,
Because two is always best,
We will wear our thick warm coats
And of course our thermal vests.

We'll climb up high mountains
And cross the deep ravines,
We'll be the greatest explorers,
The world has ever seen!

Sheila Gee

Little Star

Every elf in Lapland had been busy for weeks, it was coming up to the most important time, and everything must be ready for Christmas. Lots of presents to make and prepare - toy tractors, trains, lorries and buses for the little boys, dolls and prams for the little girls, bicycles to paint. The silk worms had been busy making the delicate cloth to ensure that every fairy doll had a pretty dress. They had to work especially hard, but do you know, they always made just enough so that every fairy doll looked beautiful. The colours for the cloth were taken from the beautiful summer rainbows, special, important fairy elves gathered the lovely colours, flying into the sky on delicate wings, climbing the rainbow, each carrying a gossamer bag to collect the colours. Lookout elves watched out for showers of rain because they knew you only got a rainbow in sunshine and showers, so they gathered while they could.

Carpenter elves had been busy also, sawing and cutting wood to make some of the toys, in fact, there was a great deal of noise in Lapland; sawing, hammering, happy elves singing as they worked. They all love preparing for Christmas. The thought of smiling children opening their presents on Christmas morning filled them with happiness, and because everyone in Lapland loved Father Christmas, it was always a pleasure to help him. He was such a happy chap, and when everything ran smoothly it meant that Christmas Day was his best day ever.

At the moment however, there was a 'Do not disturb' sign on his door; Father Christmas was sleeping. He needed quite a lot of sleep, he could be heard snoring very loudly. The sound made some of the elves smile, especially the younger ones. The thing was, Father Christmas was very old. He had been making the long journey every Christmas Eve for many years. His old bones ached and his beard had grown longer and whiter, but he knew that he would carry on taking presents to the children as long as he lived, and that would be forever.

There were other important jobs that always needed doing at this time of year. The sleigh needed a good clean; it was stored in the barn every year after each trip, dusty and covered in cobwebs, in need of painting. The elves took it in turn to do this job. The elves who didn't like spiders were excused this work. It was usually the young ones but secretly some of the old elves thought it an excuse not to do the work but because elves are kind, they didn't grumble, they just got on with it.

Meanwhile, Rudolph and the other reindeer who had been put out to pasture all summer were being prepared for the long journey. They had lazed, and grazed all summer, but it was now time to go on a few short trips to exercise and get into shape. They needed it, eating and sleeping had made them lazy. Dancer and Blitzen, who it was known, tended to eat too much, had such fat tummies that their harnesses were too tight, so it was extra exercise for them. A few trips round the back of the moon soon had them nice and slim. And it went without saying that a trip around the back of the moon was always an adventure. You never knew what you might find. The elves loved it so taking Dancer and Blitzen for their exercise was a pleasure. The back of the moon was magic. Oh yes, it was very dark, but it wasn't really scary. At certain times you were able to see pretty lights, and mysterious noises could be heard. Nice noises, lovely distant music that seemed to float on the night air. The older, wiser elves said there were many things in the vast emptiness beyond the moon. Many stars and planets, and who knows, there may even be places where other elves and reindeer lived and other worlds full of different people. Father Christmas used to smile to himself when he listened to the tales that the old elves told the youngsters, and the look in his gentle eyes spoke of knowing many things. Well, he had been around for a very long time.

As the elves worked, each one knew the job he must do. Carpenters cut wood, nailing each piece together until it made a tractor, truck, or any one of the many toys they produced. Painters prepared the pots of paint, stirring and selecting each colour, bright red for the tractors and fire engines. One day a young elf painted a fire engine pale pink, it was very soon rubbed down by one of the older elves. 'My goodness,' the oldest elf said. 'I don't think little boys would like pink engines!' It was agreed he was probably right. Everyone had a good laugh except for the young elf who had painted the tractor pink. He had quite liked the colour. Father Christmas had noted the little elf's disappointment. He'd smiled and nodded to himself. He would make sure the little elf wasn't sad for too long.

Christmas Eve was approaching fast, Father Christmas kept a close eye on the work being done. He admired the elves for the long hours they put in, everyone working so hard to make sure that everything was ready for the big day, not minding the extra time. They were a good bunch, and he would make sure that they had the usual reward.

Father Christmas looked out of the window. *Is that snow? It could be? I hope it is.* He walked over to his door. He loved snow, especially on

Christmas Eve, riding on the sleigh through the night sky with snow falling gently always gave him a buzz. To land on the snow-covered rooftops with a loaded sleigh full to overflowing with sacks full of toys for the children was such a joy and to see Rudolph's bright red nose glowing so bright, forming a shaft of light guiding them all the way from Lapland to the rooftops of the world was brilliant. He loved it. Everything about Christmas was great. Father Christmas knew he was childish, but he didn't care, although, if he was honest, it had been easier in the olden days to deliver the presents. When every home had a coal fire and a big chimney. He recalled the days when he had to sit on some rooftops waiting for the fire to go out before he could deliver the presents. He remembered one Christmas Eve having to wait ages for one huge fire to go out, and in his haste, because he was running late, he had gone down the very hot chimney and burnt his bum. Good job it was the last house and he was able to go home to Mother Christmas who put cream and a bandage on the burns. He was soon right as rain. He had been a bit worried though when most people seemed to have central heating and many houses no longer had a chimney, as coal fires went out of fashion. It made it difficult for him to deliver Christmas presents. One clever elf had invented a magic golden key that would open any door. Now, Rudolph could land on the rooftops, and if it had been snowing Father Christmas could slide down the roofs, use the magic key, and leave the presents that way. Wasn't that exciting!

What wasn't so exciting however, and what was concerning was; whilst the elves were preparing Rudolph for the long journey, they realised that his light was very dull, and it didn't matter how they tried, it wouldn't brighten. The electrician elf examined Rudolph's nose. He poked it, prodded it, squeezed it, making poor Rudolph yell, but no matter how they tried, the light remained dull and Rudolph began to cry. 'How will I ever find my way without my bright red nose to light my path? I've let Father Christmas down,' and Rudolph put his head down and turned to walk away.

All the worried elves went to see Father Christmas. They didn't want to upset him but this was serious. No light, no Christmas presents. As they talked over the situation, the youngest elf spoke up. 'I know, I know! Do you remember the long journey to the Goodlux factory last year, to get red paint?' All the elves looked at each other.

'Yes,' said the oldest elf, 'then we went delivering Christmas presents, and when we came back Rudolph was put out to pasture. All the power in his nose was used up and he didn't get a recharge, and there isn't time now! We won't be going anywhere this Christmas.' Rudolph continued to sob.

Meanwhile, the Star of the East was on his usual journey. He had travelled the vast sky since time began, but two thousand years ago, he had been needed to shine the way to the stable where Baby Jesus had been born. He was the greatest star of all and shone his light to show the way for weary travellers and visitors. First to arrive were the wise men and the shepherds as they went to see the Baby Jesus. There wasn't another star as important as the Star of the East. Now there was another star who had been floating around the sky for quite a number of years. He didn't feel important at all. How could he be important? He was too little, nobody took any notice of him. The bigger stars laughed. He was a little nobody … but his chance to shine was just around the corner.

As he was floating over Lapland, feeling fed up and sad he thought he could hear someone crying. He listened. Was it the wind? No, there was definitely someone crying. So Little Star went towards the weeping noise. As he looked down, he could see Father Christmas and the Lapland elves standing round a weeping deer. Little Star went closer. It was Rudolph. 'Rudolph, up here, what is it?'

The sad little deer looked to where the twinkly voice was coming from. 'My nose is dull and I can't see my way to take the presents to all the children.'

Little Star started to beam. He floated down to where Rudolph and the others were. At last, this was his chance and in a twinkle-twinkle way he started to sing …

'Gentle Rudolph please don't cry,
I've come to light your way,
Between your ears I'll nestle,
To shine as bright as day.'

As the proud little star nestled comfortably between Rudolph's ears, it seemed that the whole of Lapland gave a cheer so loud that it could be heard all over the world. Clever Little Star.

'Ho, ho, ho,' said a very happy Father Christmas. As for Rudolph and the other reindeer, well they were over the moon with happiness. Now all the children would receive their presents.

Rudolph raised his eyes towards where Little Star was snuggled, gave a big sigh of happiness, and said, 'Thank you Little Star.'

Dorothy M Mitchell

The Dugawoppy

No stairs to climb, it's such a shame
No floors to jump on, who's to blame?
Where are the walls and such and so?
Where does a Dugawoppy go?

She'd like a bed - a chair would do,
And cup and plate in palest blue.
She needs a skirt, or some such thing.
What can a Dugawoppy bring?

She's got a toothbrush and a comb,
But there's no place to call her home.
She lost her way last Tuesday week.
Where can a Dugawoppy sleep?

She's very clean; there are no smells.
She's always quiet, and never yells.
She will not slurp, or *jaw, jaw, jaw.*
She won't make messes on the floor.

Can you go home and plead her cause?
Can she please come along to yours?
Tell them of this good, kind creature,
They would really love to meet her.

Let's go and find her right away
And let her know that she can stay.

Gail Hare

Stripey The Zebra

(Written especially for Olivia King)

Stripey lived at Paignton Zoo with his mother and father, two sisters and two brothers. He was a very happy zebra, and loved to enjoy himself and have fun. During the springtime he liked to play in the big field with his family. They'd have races running round and round, and then they'd trot up and down, shaking their heads, and sometimes curling back their lips to show large powerful teeth; just right for grinding up roots and bark. Then they'd stand companionably together, cooling off under the shade of the enormous chestnut tree. Its pretty candle-like flowers were deep pink, and when a gentle breeze blew, the blossom floated down and settled on their backs and heads like confetti. Sometimes it landed on their noses, making them twitch their nostrils and laugh. They had their own comfortable wooden house to sleep in when the nights were cold, and were looked after very well by their kind keeper.

Stripey liked the visitors who came to the zoo. In summer there were hundreds winding their way across the front of his home. In winter there were a lot less, but crowds and crowds during the Christmas holidays, when Santa was in his grotto at the other end of the zoo. He'd often wondered who Santa Claus was. He knew he was very kind to all the children, giving them presents. He didn't give anything to the adults though, except mince pies, and sometimes he'd be offered a piece of one. But he didn't like it, he'd much rather be offered a nice clump of juicy grass or tempting leaves.

Best of all, Stripey loved the children. He'd push his nose forward to them when they stood to admire him, and his eyes would grow soft. Everyone talked about his smart stripe pattern coat. When he asked his mother about it, she said it acted as a camouflage, that it blended with the scenery in Africa, where he came from, so his enemies couldn't see him easily. But his dad said it helped to keep him cool. Then proudly he added, 'Each one of us has a different striped coat. It's to help us recognise each other.'

One summer evening when his family had gone to bed early, Stripey wasn't tired. He was standing contentedly under the chestnut tree when he noticed a broken fence panel, which led to a gap in the hedge at the back of his field. Being young and curious, and ready for any adventures, he followed his nose, and walked out, finding himself in a lane. Looking all around, there was no one about, and he half wondered whether he should turn back. What if he got lost? Just how brave was he?

The sky was full of stars and an owl hooted down at him. 'Don't go, little Stripey, it's not wise. Stay with your family.' And of course, his advice had just the opposite effect. *I'll just go and explore a little way,* Stripey thought to himself. *I'm sure I won't get lost.*

And so he strolled uncertainly up the lane, looking to the left and right and promising himself that he wouldn't go far. He went past where the giraffe lived, and they looked down on him in surprise, wondering where he was going. Then he came to the lion house, and here his courage nearly failed him. He knew a brand new lion cub, Lancelot, had been born recently, and that his parents were fiercely protective of him. But he couldn't go back now, so he took a deep breath and hurried on. Before he knew it, and he didn't know how, he was outside the zoo. Shock ... amazement ... disbelief - and excitement. Stripey couldn't believe it. Hundreds of shiny things on wheels, following one behind the other, and some showing a yellow blinking eye before turning off to the left and right. One seemed to have a cold, making a loud spluttering sound, with no energy to keep up with the others. Then there was a strange, impatient hooting sound, but not like the owls at the zoo made.

He thought how big the stars were here, and how strange that they all seemed to come out together, and they were held up by tall poles; perhaps they didn't have much energy either. There were lots of people hurrying about with parcels, just like the ones he saw at the zoo at Christmas, but it wasn't Christmas, it was summer.

He was wondering which way to go, when a light shower of rain started to fall. Oh, how refreshing it was. He felt the clear drops on his mane, and tufted tail, felt them slide down his stripes, and putting out his tongue, he closed his eyes, the more to enjoy them. And then it happened!

A little girl, who seemed to be alone, carrying a basket, was about to run into the road, to cross over, Stripey at once saw the danger, and without thinking of his own safety, he hurried over to her, and out into the road to stop the traffic. But somehow he slipped. There was a screeching of brakes, and lots of shouting. And then he felt a pain in his head and his back, and he lay quite still.

He woke up in the animal hospital, and he was a hero. He'd saved the child's life, and apart from a terrible headache, and an aching back, the doctor told him that he'd be alright.

The little girl was called Olivia, and she and her mother came to visit Stripey, to thank him for being so brave. Olivia gave him a great big kiss, and he nuzzled his striped head against her pink cheek.

His family were so proud of him, and everyone in the zoo was so proud of him. All the animals wanted to see him, so they could cheer him, and as he passed where they lived, they'd bang their tails on the ground, or squawk; some even blew him kisses.

A few days later a large sign was erected outside the zoo gates, proudly proclaiming *Stripey, the Brave lives here.*

I expect you've crossed the road on zebra crossings. They've been put there to show you it's a safe place to cross. And now you know how they got there!

Gloria Thorne

Moles

(For Merry Millie, Cheerful Charlotte and Happy Harry)

Moles dig holes.
Everybody knows moles dig holes,
and some moles dig holes faster than others.

Some moles have dug so many holes
they're into double digits.
The fastest double-digit digger
is undoubtedly our Doug.

Doug digs double-digit holes so fast
he digs it (and it's made to last)
before other diggers even start.
Many diggers think it is because
he's got a bigger ticker.

The whole hole-digging brotherhood,
had a competition
to see who was the fastest double-digit digger
in the whole hole-digging community.

Doug and many others started digging double-digit holes.
The other double-digit hole-diggers
were demoralized from the start.
Our Doug was digging diligently,
sure he was going to win.

Doug was still doggedly digging
When he found he was backed up
against the backside of Brock the Badger.
Brock the Badger's brush was blocking
Doug's double-digit digging race -
and poor Doug lost!

But everyone knew he would have won
if Brock the Badger's brush hadn't blocked
Doug's double-digit digging.

David Walter

The Little Train

A smart little train all shiny and clean
Could not move as it had run out of steam
I know that this story sounds cruel
This smart little train had run out of fuel
Along came a man with some coal in a sack
Said, 'This will soon get you back on the track'
The little train's boiler was soon well alight
Filled it with water using a hosepipe
Soon steam was puffing out of its stack
Now the little train can run forwards and back
Still bright and shiny and still very clean
Our little train now has lots of steam.

L A G Butler

The Oh So Big Moth

How do we react, when out of nowhere
an Oh! so big moth appears?
Flapping around the light, around your head and in your ears!
We dart around hysterically, jumping here and there,
trying your best to catch it before it goes God only knows where!
You know you're going to have to kill it, just to give you peace
of mind,
but this moth is Oh! so big and you are not really the hunting kind.
You put on your rubber gloves and get a cloth or two,
might as well get a long pole, anything and everything will do.
You shut yourself in the room with it poised and ready to fight.
Oh no! Don't land on the ceiling, now it's up into the light.
I can hear my family laughing, but I must make a stand,
so, it's a bit unexpected when my husband appears, his arm uplifted
and caught it in his hand!
His hand . . . urgh!
He took it to the front door and opened it to let him fly,
I shouted after it, 'Come back again and prepare to die!'
I wanted to have the last word, to tell him I wasn't going soft,
but I know in my heart I'm really so glad I didn't have to catch that Oh!
so big moth!

Mary Plumb

Fly By Night

I looked up at the sky one night
And saw a saucer burning bright.
I gaped in awe not believing my eyes,
As it spun and danced in the navy skies.

This was a spectre I'd read about,
And here it was without a doubt.

Quick as I could,
I ran to the phone,
To see if I'd find a scientist home.

'Cause it was rather late,
Or was it early?
At three in the morning
They might have got surly.

Then they arrived an hour before dawn,
Then congregated fast on the lawn.
They had glasses perched
On the end of their noses;
And a cameraman trod
A path through the roses.

The neighbours to whom
I don't usually chat,
Opened their windows
And cried, 'What's all that?'

On seeing the crowd that
Now milled with excitement
Looking up at the sky
(Waiting for enlightenment).

'Pardon me dear,' one important man said,
'B'lieve you saw the . . . er . . . saucer
Fly over your head?
Think I'll take a few details,
May I please step inside?'
We walked to the door that was opened wide.

The cameras looked on bright
And friendly,
The microphones were put in place;
Reporters flocked to ask me questions,
What was this 'thing' from outer space?

The scientists were still outside
And marked its route up in the sky.
It had flown behind Pluto,
And then perhaps Venus -
It avoided Uranus . . . My oh my.

This hubbub continued
For several long hours,
Then the best of the event
Happened later that day;
We all saw the saucer
Circling slowly . . .
When a flying cup sat on it
And they both flew away!

Gabriela Alexander

The China Doll Called Sally

Standing on the window sill was this beautiful china doll. It had been a present to a little girl named Sian from her great auntie Joy on her Daddy's side of the family. The doll must be at least fifty years old and Sian wouldn't part with her! It was the doll she had called Sally.

'Mummy, do you think Sally would miss me if she got lost?' Sian looked straight into her mummy's eyes.

'How would Sally get lost? She hasn't been moved from the window sill since Auntie Joy gave her to you. Why do you say that dear? It's a very funny thing to say.' Doris thought Sian was growing up too quick, she seemed to have an old head on young shoulders.

'I had a dream last night, I woke and thought Sally had gone,' said Sian, who was coming up to her fourth birthday and perhaps was getting excited about the party Mummy and Daddy were planning for her.

'We all have dreams dear, they don't mean anything, just try and forget.' Doris then took Sian's hand and led her into the garden.

Several years later, Sian, by this time seven years of age, had settled into her school very nicely and Doris was very pleased with her progress. Also, Sian seemed really happy each day going off to school. Sian still had Sally sitting on the window sill, and still talked to her every night before she went to sleep. She had never forgotten the dream although she never told Mummy about it, and every morning she was so pleased to find her china doll still sitting there.

One day she decided to take Sally to school, this was a day when the children were encouraged to bring a special toy to school to show their teacher. This happened only one day a year and the teacher gave over one lesson to the children and their toys.

Sian was excited to show her Sally off because she had never taken her to school before. She knew she would have to be very careful with her, because it would break her heart if anything bad happened.

'That is a very pretty doll,' said Miss Foster, 'how long have you had her?'

'I've had her for years, my great auntie Joy gave her to me.' Sian was delighted that her form teacher had noticed Sally.

'She must be quite valuable, so look after her.' Miss Foster walked away.

Sian suddenly felt the fear return of the dream all those years ago and put her hands firmly around precious Sally.

Forward Press - Take A Peek . . .

The day passed and when it was time to go home all the children ran out to their parents safe in the knowledge that there had been no accidents with their toys. Sian told her mum all about the exciting day that she'd had and that Miss Foster had taken particular notice of Sally. Mum said that was very nice and after Sian finished her tea, Sally was placed safely on the window sill. She climbed into bed.

It was about six-thirty the next morning when Sian woke and looked over at the window sill. She sat upright in her bed. 'Mum, Sally's gone,' Sian was screaming and her mum came running up the stairs and was upset to see Sian in a dreadful state.

'What is the matter dear?' Doris sat Sian down on her bed, put her arms around her.

'Mummy, look, Sally has gone.'

'Is that all, calm down, I know where she is.'

'Where?'

'Downstairs on the sideboard, when you took her to school yesterday I noticed on her return that she looked ever so slightly dirty.' Doris immediately saw Sian change, she hadn't really realised that Sian put so much importance on her doll. 'You go down and bring her upstairs, you will see the difference.'

Sian went downstairs and there her precious Sally stood and what a clean doll she was.

A great many years went by and Sian grew into a beautiful young lady, and attended Ravensworth College for Girls. She was getting excellent results and looking forward to achieving enough passes for university. Doris was really proud of the way she had grown up. Sian still had Sally on the window sill but the difference was she didn't panic if Sally was missing anymore, you see she also had a younger sister and while she was being grown up, her sister Clare was looking after the china doll named Sally.

Iris Crew

Dad

There is a man whom I call Dad.
I know there are many,
        But that isn't bad,
For this one Dad, the one I call,
Is better than most,
        No! Better than all.

For he is my Dad, the one with that laugh;
He creases his eyes up and blurts out a sound,
He cackles a little,
        Then a noise, quite profound;

It gurgles and yelps like a ticklish drain,
Then another big chortle,
        The tears pour, not in vain,
For all of his being is lost in this grin,
So contagiously silly,
        We all must join in.

We cackle and gurgle
        And shout with delight,
Our faces are aching,
        We laugh through the night.

And by the time the morning light comes
We try to remember,
        We try to recall,
What was ever so funny that made us laugh so,
        At all!

Joanna Wallfisch

Keys

I like keys, I do
I'd like a set for Christmas too
If I was bigger, I could reach the table
Once up there, then I'd be able
To listen to the *jingle, jangle* noise
Far, far better than my boring toys
But my parents spoil all my fun
It's sad and lonely, being only one!

Lisa Knight

Snooks

A simple little duck am I
And not too good on looks.
But to my mistress, I'm her pet,
Her precious little 'Snooks'.

I follow her around the house
Directing all her chores.
And when she goes to feed the ducks,
I follow her outdoors.

The other ducks don't like me much,
When I'm around they quack.
Their angry words just drop away
Like water off my back.

It doesn't bother me at all
The way they groan and grouse.
I wave my little tail at them,
Then walk back to the house.

I don't feel like a duck at all
I'm Snooks, a little pet.
In fact I don't like water much
And my feet are never wet.

If *duck* is on the menu
As a special treat for tea,
I'm not so sure of those outside,
But I know it won't be me.

Colleen Simons

The Policeman Who Couldn't Sleep

Once upon a time in an old city called Gloucester, a young policeman tried hard to get to sleep in his room on the top floor of the police station. Oh how he tried! Every night it was the same, the seagulls flew squawking overhead. Round and round they flew. Sometimes their cry was like the cruel laugh of a wicked witch. 'Ha-ha-ha-ha-ha!' they went. Other times their sound was like a gentle mewing, rather like the soft cry of a young child. Yet again they might make a variety of noises, rather like a conversation between two human beings.

'This won't do,' said the young policeman. 'It simply will not do. I need my sleep - everyone needs a good sound sleep and I am not sleeping *at all!*' The policeman was angry. He was good-looking and his uniform was clean and tidy. He looked fine in his helmet, but when he hadn't slept his helmet weighed heavily on his head, which ached and throbbed with fatigue. Whatever could he do? He wanted to be a sergeant and he was only a constable. Later on he wanted to be an inspector or even a chief constable. How could he climb up the steep police ladder of promotion with no proper sleep, he wondered? Only yesterday he had filled in the wrong forms while on duty at the enquiry desk. Last Monday he had tried to get into the patrol car wearing his helmet, instead of a flat cap, and the helmet had simply rolled into the road like a rugby ball.

On Wednesday he had put on his football socks instead of his black ones and they were red and white striped and looked very odd with his dark uniform. And he'd nearly forgotten his notebook and pencil this morning. Whatever next? It simply would not do.

Then he had an idea. In order to escape the seagulls he would have to return to his parents' house in Cheltenham. There it was peaceful. No seagulls cried or hopped about on the chimney pots cackling with crazy laughter. Yes, that's what he'd do. He'd go back home and live in peace with his father and mother and younger brothers. It was the only way forward, that's for sure. So the young policeman packed his suitcases and went home and lived happily ever after.

Mary Hinksman

Gollipotti People

Down in Gollipotti, by the Gollipotti Sea,
Live the Gollipotti people who are very strange to see.
They wear Gollipotti clothes with Gollipotti hats,
And sitting by their fires there are Gollipotti cats.

Their week begins on Tuesdays, and ends on Monday night,
They sleep throughout the daytime and sometimes all the night.
Gollipottis look peculiar; they have a long hooked nose,
They measure only two-feet high and wear bright purple clothes.

Their shoes are hollowed acorns, from the Molliwoddi trees
And they wear bright purple breeches that come down to their knees.
The skins of yellow pumpkins, Gollipottis have for hats,
Tiny gloves upon their hands are made from wings of bats.

Gollipottis don't get married; it's very strange you see,
Because Gollipotti babies grow on Molliwoddi trees.
They wave about on branches and cry and shout, and sing,
Then when they are just four months old they fall off in the spring.

When Gollipottis collect them it is a funny sight,
For waving in the sun for months, a few are over ripe.
Babies on the shady side are really underdone,
The Gollipottis put them back to get a bit more sun.

Monday is their shopping day and Gollipotti streets
Are full of rows of houses made of Gollipotti sweets.
It is a funny sight to see; in fact it looks quite queer,
Because the Gollipottis lick and chew until they disappear.

When the Gollipottis sleep, in the middle of the night,
Shopkeepers build them back again with chocolate and spice.
The walls are made of candy bars covered with sweet honey,
With rooftops made from chocolate coins called artificial money.

Gollipottis don't use motor cars; they think them quite absurd,
They fly around upon the back of the Celepitie bird.
When he's running down the runway on his yellow spindly legs,
The Gollipottis bump and toss and fall off on their heads.

Gollipottis' pets are snow-white, pink-eyed giant rats,
And they pull them though the streets on yellow pumpkin traps.
Gollipotti is a peaceful place, no noises can be heard,
With yellow pumpkin carriages and the Celepitie bird.

Forward Press - Take A Peek . . .

On their sports day in the stadium, it does seem rather queer,
For instead of running round a circle, they run around a square.
They run round anti-clockwise, at each corner turn sharp right,
With those sharp turns, and bright clothes what a funny sight.

Gollipottis on the high jump do not play quite fair,
They put springs in their plimsolls and vanish in the air.
Like a red space rocket they shoot into the sky,
Then all round Gollipotti like a satellite they fly.

The team which they compete with, from an island in the north,
Are called the Cupperwuddies and they're very good at sport.
They're all so athletic and their legs are long and thin.
The Gollipottis find it very difficult to win.

Then all of the winners have a scrumptious chocolate cup,
They hold a winner's party and they quickly eat them up.
When a Cupperwuddie beats them it isn't a disgrace,
For in the land of Gollipotti the slowest wins the race.

Gollipottis go to school to learn to read and write,
They write from right to left instead of left to right.
Before school commences, in assembly in the hall,
To their god called Mo they shout and sing and bawl.

Mo's a giant pumpkin to whom they shout and sing,
It sounds like church Latin, but it's Gollipotti hymns.
Mo; mighty yellow pumpkin from Heaven in the ground,
To their mighty god Mo they raise a mighty sound.

They don't go down the street, Gollipottis go round and round,
Their houses form a circle and stand twelve feet from the ground.
In the middle of the circle stands a temple for Mighty Mo,
Their holy day is Wednesday, when to worship Mo they go.

To a large yellow pumpkin Gollipottis' voices raise,
Ho! Mighty Mo. Oh wonderful Mo! They sing their song of praise.
Toward the end of the service a Gollipotti priest,
Cuts the pumpkin into slices for a Gollipotti feast.

Mighty Mo! Wonderful Mo! The Gollipottis sing,
Reward us for being good, and forgive us for our sins.
When a Gollipotti dies all Gollipottis raise a sound,
'Ho! Mighty Mo, please take him to your Heaven in the ground.'

For adventure they sail on the Gollipotti Sea,
In a tall ship that is made from a Molliwoddi tree.
Tossed high upon the waves, they sometimes spring a leak,
Then sink to the bottom of the Gollipotti deep.

Their hats are often left behind, they are such a funny sight,
Because those yellow pumpkin hats can give the fish a fright.
They look just like flying saucers, arrived from outer space,
Or lots of yellow fish they call Gollipotti plaice.

A painted red tall ship with an orange flag displayed,
Is guided through the sea, by Gollipotti mermaids.
Fastened to their arms are delicate golden thongs,
And they swim to the rhythm of the Gollipotti songs.

'Ho! Beautiful fair mermaids pull this ship for me,
Tossing up and down on the Gollipotti Sea.
Take us back to paradise, and enchantment when we land,
Safely home, and happy back on golden Gollipotti sand.'

Edward L G Holmes

Untitled

A wombat called Freddie liked football
Attending each Saturday game
He only liked rough games and punch-ups
The rest were so boring and tame

He shouted so loud at the players
'Come on boys, kick 'em real hard!'
The referee stopped all proceedings
And handed out Fred a red card!

John Francis

The Darkness Hours

Still dark outside
my eyes hide
the shadowy terrors
that lurk, ready.
I hold steady
as eyelids lift
a fraction.
No reaction.
Am I OK?

Tension. The ear
alert to hear
the faintest sound
behind my head.
Dead still in bed
I lie.
Tap-tap on pane,
is that rain?
Body rigid: I'm OK.

Breathing stilled.
Room is filled
with moving air
across my cheek.
I cannot keep
my fear at bay.
Throat so dry
I need to try
and swallow; OK.

Eyes now wide
see shadows slide
across the wall.
Fear takes hold
heart beats cold
in chest. But
light switch near
remove the fear
it drums; OK.

Now gazing round
but nothing found,
untoward.
Curtains blowing,
moonlight glowing
on wind-tossed rain.
All now explained.
Demons restrained.
Back to sleep; OK.

Sandra Griesbach

The Trolls

The boys were on holiday, they had taken a stroll before dinner down to some rocky caves on the coastline.

A voice boomed out from one of the caves. 'I'm down here little ones, come and see me, I've lots of goodies to eat.'

Simon and Michael looked at one another in amazement. 'What do we do?' asked Simon.

They were both frightened and curious and exceedingly hungry.

'Run for it,' replied a more cautious Michael.

Their curiosity was compelling them to take a look in the cave.

'Won't harm you,' said the voice. 'I get lonely down here with no one to talk to except Mrs Troll.'

'What are you doing in a cave?' said Simon.

'I live down here, I'm what you call a troll.'

'A troll,' echoed the boys. 'We read about them in books or heard stories about them, we did not think that creatures like you existed.'

'Come in and take a look for yourselves,' answered the troll.

The boys crept closer.

'Do not be afraid, I am eating my dinner in the corner here, come and join me, it's a good stew made by my wife Hildeberg.'

There was a sort of a grunt from the other side of the cave and a creature with long tangled matted hair lurched forward. She had a long pointed face, with an even longer nose, with a bump on it. Her hands were large with long fingernails. She put two plates on the table. The food looked and smelled delicious and they were very hungry too. They looked at one another.

'Shall we try it?' said Simon.

They tasted the stew. They were sat up, and alive, it was good. The boys gobbled on. Hildeberg kept prodding and poking at Michael, as if he was a meat joint.

'There's not much meat on them bones,' she said, 'scraggily urchin he be.'

'Leave my bones alone,' protested Michael.

'She never had a little troll and she always has a good feel,' interceded Stanislaf.

Michael became very uneasy and signalled to his friend to move.

'Thanks for the food but we really must go, our parents are taking us out, nice meeting you.' (Nothing furthest from the truth.) They got up to bid a hasty retreat.

Suddenly the trolls were upon them, they overpowered the boys and tied them up.

'We haven't had our dessert yet dear,' said Stanislaf, 'what shall it be or should I say who should it be?'

'What, are you going to do? Eat us?' said Simon.

'Only part of you with honey, yes roasted arm and honey. It will take a few days to eat your friend,' replied Stanislaf.

'I'm thirsty dear, can we have our fruit cup?'

The fruit cup must have been very potent for both trolls fell asleep within a matter moments.

'Now's our chance.' Simon had managed to untie his hands and was quickly undoing Michael, who was by now dithering in fright. 'Come on, run for it,' urged Simon.

On the way they fell across two large boxes in their haste, there were coins in them, this was the money that had been stolen from the villagers nearby, the news had been in the local paper. The boys took one each and hurried from the cave to safety.

What a tale they had to tell their parents and everyone who would listen.

As for the trolls, they had fallen into a pack of hungry wolves, gobbled up and never seen again. So if you happen to be out exploring caves be careful, you might end up as a tasty meal. *Watch out for the trolls!*

Ellen Spring

Lennox And Friends

My name is Lennox, and I lived with my human family. I went to live with them when I was six weeks old. The lady of the house was very kind and lovely, but I think the master of the house was not too happy at first. The lady loved me an awful lot. She used to take me out every morning and evening for walks. I would do my business like a good dog.

One day my mistress was sick. She told me she was having a baby. This reminded me of when I was in my mummy's tummy, until I was born with my brothers and sisters.

Very soon, my mistress had her baby, it was a little girl. She was tiny like me. When she was in the bath, my mistress would let me sit beside the bath and watch her play. The baby was very beautiful. As time passed, my mistress still loved me, and used to take me out with the baby for long walks. We would call and visit her mother, who would always pick me up and cuddle me. She would also rub my nose, and call me pet. Then she would wash her hands and hold the baby.

I forgot to tell you, her name was Nathania Caitlin. I could never say all that. I was still a little dog, but everyone loved her too.

Sometimes Nanna would look after me and Nathania, while my new family went shopping, to buy my dog food and food for themselves. I was always good for Nanna, and Nathania would be asleep in her pram.

Soon we both grew a little older. I stayed at home, and Nathania went to stay with Nanna while Mum and Dad went to work. I now call them these names, and so does Nathania.

Soon it was time for Nathania to go to school. I just went out in the mornings and at night-times for a walk with my mistress (Mum). I started to feel poorly as I grew up. I had a lump in my groin.

They went on holiday, and I was left with another lady in kennels. There were other animals there too. One day the lady noticed my lump had grown, so she called the vet to take a look at me. The vet told her she should tell my mum to take me to our own vet to get some help. When my mum and dad returned from holiday, they took me to our vet, because they knew I was in pain. The vet said I should have the lump taken out, because in time I would be really poorly. They left me with the others and I had the operation. I was very sore after and could not walk.

Nanna looked after me for a couple of days, but I knew it made her sad to see me so poorly. So Topo (Mum's brother-in-law) came to look after me. Soon I was really ill, not eating or drinking because I could not swallow. My family took me back to the vets. There I was put to sleep because I was so ill.

I am at peace in Heaven, with my friend Hamish and all the other animals who were ill.

I know my family are very sad, but time will heal. I know they will always remember me forever.

Dilys Hallam

Squiggle And Peep

Squiggle was busy looking under the leaves, he was happily collecting the nuts that had blown down in last night's storm, and they were plentiful this autumn.

He found himself a secret store, but this meant climbing the telegraph pole and crossing the wires, he would go a short way along the wires until he came to a beech tree. The tree stood a little way back so it meant that Squiggle had to leap from the wires to the tree, this did not take a lot of effort as squirrels are fond of leaping around. He would then scurry down the tree, along the ground until he came to the steps of an old house, he would scamper up the steps and at the top he would look around to see if anyone was watching where he went. When he was certain that he was perfectly safe, he would run round to the back of the house, from there he only had a few more yards to go until he came to an old oak tree, he then ran up the tree and disappeared into the centre.

Although the tree looked like any other tree it was, in fact, quite different, it grew branches and leaves like any other tree but the centre was hollow and right inside was a metal safe. It had been hidden there a few years ago by two burglars, they had taken the safe to the old house to break it open and empty it of all the contents, then they had lowered the safe into the old tree to hide the evidence. This was an ideal place for Squiggle to hide his nuts, berries and seeds, so that he would have plenty of food for the winter.

Squiggle had come across the safe place by accident, he was on his way up the oak tree to pick some acorns, when suddenly everything went dark. He had fallen down through the middle of the tree, after he had collected his thoughts he started to look around, then he noticed some light which he ran towards, it was a small opening down near the roots of the tree. It took Squiggle a short while to work out what had happened to him, he sat for a while near the opening and looked towards the top of the tree, then he ran up the outside of the tree again and pulled up sharply, because he almost made the same mistake as before. It was then that he noticed that there was no centre to the tree, he looked down inside, although it was very dark he could just make his way back to the bottom again and it was then that he noticed this strange object which was the safe.

After cautiously investigating he saw that the door was hanging off, but that did not matter to Squiggle, as all he wanted was a safe place to store his nuts for the winter, and this would be the ideal place.

'I will have to be careful,' Squiggle muttered, 'I do not want anyone else to see where I put my rations.'

About two weeks went by and Squiggle had made himself quite snug for the winter, he had collected quite a lot of food, made himself a warm cosy bed out of dry leaves and some lambs' wool that he had collected off the barbed wire fences, but he thought he would just go out and get a few more nuts to be sure he had enough.

Well about the middle of the afternoon he was on his way back to his secret place, loaded up with more nuts. He climbed the telegraph pole and was just about to run along the wires when he gasped with shock, which made him drop all the nuts he was carrying, the sight that had caused the shock was a young jackdaw and he was hanging upside down on the wires.

Squiggle was not sure what to do, had the jackdaw fainted or was he dead? He shook his head at the last thought, *surely not, he can't be, oh no, this is dreadful,* he thought to himself, *he is so young too, who will tell his mother.* Terrible pictures began to flash through Squiggle's mind, he was just about to go and tell the other jackdaws about the tragedy when he noticed the young jackdaw looking at him through a half squinted eye, then the jackdaw started to giggle, 'Ha ha, that fooled you!'

Squiggle felt a little embarrassed at first and then he was angry, he remembered all the nuts he had dropped and how long it had taken him to collect them. 'I do not think that was very funny at all,' said Squiggle, 'I thought you were ill or dead, I did not know what I was going to tell your mother.'

When Squiggle mentioned the jackdaw's mother, the smile fell from his face. 'My mother,' gasped the jackdaw, 'please don't tell her or I will be in for a good telling off, you see I promised her I would not hang upside down on the wires again. It's just that I like doing it, it's a lovely feeling, but I am always getting told off for it. The other jackdaws say it is not natural to hang upside down, one of them called me a daft bat and Mother asked him what he meant by it, and he said bats hang upside down and any jackdaw that did it must be daft.'

Squiggle felt a little sorry for the young jackdaw after he heard this. 'Well,' he said, 'I think the other jackdaws are very unkind and not at all understanding, after all it would not do for us all to be the same, and life would be very dull if we were.'

'Oh thank you,' said the young jackdaw, 'it is nice to meet someone who is a little sympathetic, by the way, what is your name?'

Squiggle told him and then asked him what his name was.

'If I tell you, promise me that you will not laugh.' The jackdaw looked a little embarrassed. Squiggle was puzzled by this statement, but he promised, but the jackdaw asked again, 'Are you sure you will not laugh?'

'Of course not, I promised didn't I?'

'Well, I am called Peep.'

The squirrel just stood there and said, 'Um, that's er, a nice name, hasn't the weather been strange lately?' the last bit of the statement was put in, in order to stifle a laugh that was building up inside him.

'You want to laugh don't you?'

'Of course not.' But Squiggle's voice was a bit high-pitched through suppressing a laugh.

'I just know that you do.'

Squiggle pushed his paw into his mouth, he tried so hard not to laugh, and after all he had promised.

'Go on Squiggle, you might just as well laugh, I will not hold you to your promise, you are already going red in the face.'

With that he went into hysterics, Peep felt very unhappy to see him laughing so hard, but he just could not help himself, after a while he did manage to pull himself together and apologised for breaking his promise.

But Peep just looked sad and moaned, 'It's alright, I know it is a funny name.'

Squiggle, fully composed asked, 'How on earth did you get a name like that?'

'Well, if I tell you, you will only start laughing again.'

Squiggle assured him that he wouldn't.

'Oh yes you will, in fact just thinking about it makes me want to laugh as well.'

'Come on, do tell.'

'All right then, I got the name because whenever Mother came to feed us when we were chicks, my brothers and sisters made so much noise, and myself, being the youngest, I was not getting as much food as the rest of them. Mother did not hear me as well as the others, so I started to get a little weak with hunger, so instead of the usual noise that young jackdaws make, I used to shout *peep, peep*, and because it was different my mother used to hear it over all the others. In fact she used to feed me first, after that I never changed it, I still say *peep, peep* when it is time for meals. I learned to hang upside down in the nest as well because as I got bigger, I became hungrier and noticed a branch just above the nest, so when I had been fed and Mother was feeding the others I used to cling to the branch and as Mother was putting food into the other chicks' beaks, I was taking some of it out again, after all I was not too well fed in the beginning.'

'That's amazing,' exclaimed Squiggle, 'did the other chicks go hungry?'

'Oh no, I only took a little bit from each one of them so no one came to any harm.'

Squiggle and Peep stood on the wires talking for some time. They became very good friends and started to clown around. Squiggle was doing his tightrope act with a hazelnut perched on the top of his head, and Peep went into his upside down act and kept saying *peep, peep*. They were giggling quite a bit when suddenly, without warning, there was a loud whoosh. Squiggle was just about to say something to Peep when the next thing he knew he was falling through the air. He could see the ground getting closer and closer, then just as suddenly he stopped falling and noticed that he was rising higher and higher and so back to safety on the wires.

Peep had seen Squiggle falling and swooped down from his upside down position and caught Squiggle with his claws and flown him back onto the wires, no sooner had they landed when there was another loud whoosh. The amazed pair stood and watched as a rook was chasing a hawk off the rook's territory, as they flew past a third time they only just missed bumping into Peep because he went into his upside down position on the wire.

'Hey!' shouted Squiggle, 'watch out you two.'

The other jackdaws had witnessed Peep saving Squiggle, and they had also noticed how cleverly he had avoided being knocked off the wires himself, so Peep was not such a daft bat after all, perhaps he could teach all the young jackdaws how to hang upside down. It might well come in handy in a crisis.

So Peep was nominated to teach all the young jackdaws, which pleased Squiggle and also the mother of Peep.

The two friends decided it had been a long day and it was time to go home, so Peep helped his new friend to collect all the nuts he had dropped earlier, then they said their goodbyes and promised to meet up the following day.

Peep went back with his mother and Squiggle went back to his little safe place, after storing his rations, he had his supper, snuggled up in his cosy bed, and fell fast asleep.

Josephine Smith

The Fox And The Grapes

Foxy was in the most terrible mood,
Completely famished from a lack of food,
Till he spied upon a field of vines,
And his eyes with greed began to shine.
Yet the juicy grapes were much too high,
And many times did Foxy try
To jump and grab the luscious treats,
But every time he met defeat,
Till in the end he stopped and said,
'I really couldn't give a shred,
Those grapes are sour and I have to say,
I wouldn't want them anyway.'

From Foxy's tale we mustn't forget,
It's easy to hate what you cannot get.

Katy Fulker

Baby Sister

I have a baby sister who has only just been born
She's little and all wrinkly and her name is to be Dawn
My mummy says she's too young to come and play with me
But I want to play now not wait a long time you see
Everybody looks at her and all of them say
'What a pretty baby, she'll be a beauty one day'
Have they forgotten I'm here and I am only three
Oh no, here comes my grandad, he will play with me.

Ann Morgan

A Flaming Thirst

Six-year-old Jamie, was safely upstairs
while his gran watched TV in the lounge, unawares.
But then Jamie came down, and asked for a drink,
'The big glass,' he said, 'would be better, I think.'

His gran gave him water, and settled once more,
then Jamie's head peeped back around the lounge door.
'I'm thirsty again!' so his gran got back up
and got him a drink, in a much bigger cup.

Five times he came down for water, and then,
Gran asked him outright, when he came down again
'Why do you need so much water in bed?'
'Cause my bedroom's still on fire!' he said.

Margaret Sanderson

Beth And Rose At Four

Once there were twin sisters
One called Beth and one called Rose
Who would always fight and argue
But then again who knows . . .

Thought their mum as yet again
She worked at cleaning up their mess
Maybe one day they'll grow up
And they'll argue less and less

Perhaps one day they'll learn to share
Play together, have a laugh
With no raised voices, sharing toys
Even in the bath

Driven to despair at times
With constant fuss and noise
As she played at being referee
Trying to be fair and share out toys

Their mum sat quietly thinking
How hard it had become
Raising two four-year-olds
And always yearning for some . . .

Peace and quiet at last she thought
As she looked in on them in bed
Sound asleep and looking gorgeous
'How I love you both,' she said.

Claire Rushbrook

Hot Soup And Hot Dogs!

Bonfire Night had always been a fixture on the Stokes' calendar and this year would be no exception. There was much flurry through the day as they not only had visitors for the bonfire but lots of food to prepare. Claire, mother of Zara and Peter and wife of Nick, was very busy indeed.

'Oh dear,' she said, as she pre-prepared food, 'I've run out of potatoes. As you are going to the village, you might bring back the drinks? I shall have to go to Aunt Hannah's house, down the road, to get some more potatoes,' she told the children.

'Yes, we'll get the drinks,' replied Zara and Peter. 'We'll be only too happy to do so.'

'Here's my list,' said Claire, handing it to them. The children were not entering their teens and were helpful, particularly as they liked Bonfire Night. They left and Claire hurried down the road, leaving the back door unlocked. She would only be away for five minutes. She had taken off her gold wedding ring to make the pastry and had left it on the kitchen sink.

Aunt Hannah had visitors so Claire was away longer than her estimated five minutes. As she hurried back she noticed that the back door was wide open. She went to go in when a young man pushed hurriedly by. She realised that he was a young burglar. She chased him, followed by the dog who caught up and nipped his heels. In fright he threw away the few small things he had collected and leapt over the low fence and disappeared. Claire collected all the pieces and small items he'd thrown away. They were near the bonfire so she was lucky to get them, intact. She was so shaken that she sat down to relax and to collect herself before carrying on with the preparations.

Zara and Peter returned with the wine. They noticed her agitation. 'What's wrong Mum?' asked Peter, concerned.

'Do you know, while I was away for that short time, a young burglar came into the house. I chased him which resulted in his throwing the small stolen items away. I've collected them.'

'How awful! What a shock for you!' said Zara, 'but luckily you were able to retrieve the stolen items.'

Claire went to the sink to wash her hands and put on her ring. She threw up her hands and shrieked, 'My ring has gone! What will I do?' Her face was pallid and one solitary tear ran down her face.

'Mum, we'll phone the police, though I doubt if they can do much as burglaries are not of prime importance to them anymore,' said Peter.

'Thank you!' said Claire, 'I must get on with the food preparation.'

In due course, the local village policeman dropped in and took down a description of the ring and that of the robber. 'A local teenager, I would think,' he said. 'We'll see what we can do.' PC Pike was a pleasant fellow and well liked in the village.

'Now, we must proceed with things. We have told Aunt Hannah and your three cousins to be here by 8 o'clock so, if you're going out, be sure to be back by then - your father, too.'

'OK!' the duo replied.

Eight pm duly arrived. It was a chilly, autumnal night - fortunately not raining. Aunt Hannah, Rose and Lawrence had arrived, also the Brown children, next door, with their parents.

Claire looked tired. 'Are you alright Mum?' Peter said, putting his arms around Claire and giving her a little squeeze.

'Yes, I'm alright,' she smiled, putting her head on his shoulder.

The 'guy' was atop the bonfire and their father lit the fire. It was already aflame and Claire stared hypnotically into the glow, watching the patterns made by the flames. 'A bit nippy,' she shivered, snuggling into her fur collar and putting on her gloves.

'Isn't it always?' Peter joked. 'Do you remember that year when our toes and fingers were frozen and we nearly had frostbite? We forgot the bonfire and went inside.'

That was probably true, Claire thought. Bonfire Night had always been a cause for celebration in their family. Nick, her husband, always built a super bonfire and Zara and Peter helped by collecting branches and stacking them on the fire.

They made the Guy from an old shirt, hat and Nick's old trousers plus a head made from an old stocking filled with straw. He was mounted on a pole and put on top of the fire. When they were young the children had enjoyed seeing the Catherine wheels spinning on the fence and the sparklers which they held in their hands, also the food, afterwards.

Claire was about to laugh at the recollection but, suddenly, she felt sad. 'I wonder if I shall ever get my ring back? However, I can't dwell on it - must live for the moment,' she whispered to herself.

Each year the bonfire was larger and the fireworks more elaborate - Roman candles spouting stars and whistles and showers of sparks lighting the night sky. Last year's party had been the best ever.

Suddenly Nick shouted, 'Ready? Countdown! Four, three, two, one!'

A deafening bang and then the yard was alight with dazzling pyrotechnics, bangs, whistles and the shrieks of fireworks, accompanied by the aah-ing from the guests. *Happy times, these*, thought Claire. She then went inside to fulfil her role as a caterer. Hot soup, hot dogs and hamburgers were prepared - all steaming hot to get the guests warmed up.

'Delicious! More!' they shouted as the food was passed around.

'Throw these potatoes into the ashes - so they'll bake!' she yelled to Nick.

'Not long to go, now, Mum.' It was Zara, at her side. She slipped her hand into hers.

'How are you doing?' Zara asked.

'Fine,' Claire nodded.

The feast having ended, Nick climbed on a chair to thank the guests. The fire had been reduced to embers. The last fireworks lit the sky. Zara bent to pick up the hot potatoes and let out a cry.

'Whatever is the matter?' asked Claire.

'It's your ring, Mum. He must have thrown it near the fire. It's black and charred but it's definitely yours.' They all circled Zara and peered at it.

Claire let a tear run down her cheek. Those present yelled, 'Bravo!'

'What a fitting finale - finding the ring!' said Zara.

Nick joined them. 'The ring looks bad but it will be quite easily fixed. Tomorrow I shall get to work and you will have your ring, as new.'

'Oh thank you,' Claire said, giving them a hug. And after they came inside there was a phone call from PC Pike. He had arrested a young lad for entering their home and for attempted burglary, and they were able to tell him that the ring had been found. What a remarkable evening it had been, in every respect!

Nola B Small

Why Is The Sky Blue?

Nathan woke up and looked out of the window. It was a bright sunny day, the birds were singing and the sky was bright blue.

Nathan could hear his mum coming upstairs, she opened the door and said, 'Come on lazy bones, get ready for school.'

Nathan gazed up at the sky, 'Mum,' he said, 'why is the sky blue?'

Mum laughed, 'Oh you do ask silly questions Nathan,' she said. 'The sky isn't always blue, sometimes it can be grey or even white with all the clouds. It's blue today because it is a lovely, warm, sunny day.'

Nathan looked puzzled, 'But why is it blue Mum?' he asked.

Mum just smiled, 'Breakfast is on the table,' she said and went downstairs.

When Nathan arrived at school he sat by the window, gazing up at the sky. Mrs Wilson was not happy. 'Nathan,' she shouted, 'I do wish you would pay attention to the lesson and stop looking out of the window.'

Everyone stared at him, and Nathan was embarrassed, his face went bright red. Mrs Wilson was teaching geography, Nathan put his hand up.

'Yes Nathan?' said Mrs Wilson.

'Miss,' he asked, 'why is the sky blue?'

Everyone giggled.

'Well,' said Mrs Wilson, 'the sky is blue because it's a sunny day and God created the Earth and made the sky blue.'

'But why isn't it red or yellow or even green?' asked Nathan.

'Well sometimes the sky is red,' said Mrs Wilson, 'if tomorrow is going to be a very warm, sunny day then the sky goes red. There is a saying, 'red sky at night, shepherds' delight'.'

Nathan still felt confused and wondered why the sky was blue.

At playtime it started to rain heavily and Matthew and Nathan were splashing about in the puddles. The bell rang. 'Everyone inside quickly,' shouted Mrs Wilson.

The rain got heavier, Nathan took his pencils out of his desk, the class were going to start an art lesson. 'Today we're going to make a windmill,' said Mrs Wilson, and put the lights on. 'Oh dear,' she said, 'the room has gone quite dark with all this rain.' Nathan looked up at the sky, it was grey and murky.

After the children had finished making their windmills the sun came out and the sky turned blue again. Nathan looked out of the window, his face gleamed with delight. Mrs Wilson went over to the window and so did all the children; across the sky was the most beautiful rainbow ever. It was red, yellow, pink, green, orange, purple and blue. 'It looks like you got your wish after all,' she said to Nathan and everybody laughed.

Julie Merdassi

The Tiger In My Bed

Sleeping in my bed I was,
When the tiger woke me up,
Not fierce
Or growling was he,
But rather, he was purring at me.
I touched his fur and felt him rattle
As his purring got louder and louder,
'Sshhh,' I said, 'you'll wake my mum and dad,
And I don't think they would like a tiger
Sat with me on my bed.'
The tiger's purr got quieter,
But then he licked my face.
'Yuk!' I said and squirreled up my nose.
'Why are you in my bedroom Mr Tiger?' I had to ask,
'I couldn't sleep,' the tiger said.
'Would you like me to read you a story?
Snuggle down and I'll tell you a tale,
It will be sure to send you to sleep.'
But the story was so good
That I fell asleep instead,
And when in the morning I awoke
The tiger had gone,
But laid next to me instead was a book,
Called 'The tiger that slept in my bed'.

C Walsh

Heavenly Bodies

Take a galaxy seat, view the Earth from afar
Sit with the gods on their hidden black star
The jewel of the universe gives them hours of joy
In a younger day nursery, their favourite toy

They sit quite contented, there's been no reason to probe
Into the life of this planet, this heavenly globe
But came a low rumbling that was more than a snore
Something was bothering first Zeus and then Thor

What's caught their attention and was raising their wrath?
It appears Earth is changing and taking an unpleasant path
Why are its colours much dimmer?
Has the azure blue lost its shimmer?

Poseidon is dispatched to search 'neath the foam
Hades to the underworld, he knows where to roam
Zeus then let out a heavenly sigh
I suppose then it's me for the air and the sky

They made their report in a couple of days
Earth's not very well, she had a malaise
A virus has developed, on her skin there's a tan
No way to get better till the removal of Man.

Charles Keeble

The Frog Prince

In the middle of the woods
where the oak tree grows
the frog prince has his throne,
and every night when the moon is full
he welcomes his princess home

Fairies dressed in rainbow gowns
sing their joyous songs
wooed by the mead both sweet and strong
fierce goblins settling down
tell their tales of times long gone

Tales of when the Earth was young
and gold could be found
strewn along the riverbeds
while diamonds sold by the pound.
'Ah, those were the days!' they sing

The frog prince sighs, 'Lady mine
would that you could stay
by my side in Paradise
then I'd love you more each day.'
Sad, the princess shakes her head
she sees day is on his way

In the middle of the woods
where the oak tree stood
the music fades away
and bluebells mourn, people say
'cause the fairies stay away.

Lila Joseph

Lyla The Ladybird

Lyla the ladybird was beautiful. There was no arguing about that - everyone said so. Buzzy the Bee turned to look at her and flew straight into a tree! Freddy the frog sat on his lily pad every day, staring lazily at her with his big green eyes, and even jealous Della the dragonfly had to admit that Lyla was indeed the most beautiful ladybird she had ever seen.

She was the brightest of reds - redder than a fire engine, and twice as shiny! There were two big beauty spots on her back too, and her eyes were black as velvet. But, because she was so beautiful, she was very, very vain. She would spend hours admiring her reflection in the pond, repeating over and over again, 'Oh, what a lovely ladybird you are - quite the most beautiful ladybird in the world!'

She forgot all about the dangers that the others had warned her about - about the children who played at hide-and-seek in the Fairy Glen. In summer, they came with their jamjars, fishing for minnows, and searching for caterpillars and ladybirds to take home in their matchboxes. It was easy to forget about the dangers when the sun was shining and the flowers were inviting her to ride their gaudy petals in the breeze, but you had to watch out.

One day, the children strayed down Lyla's path. Buzzy the bee hummed as loud as he could warn her - Freddy the frog croaked and croaked, and Della the dragonfly flapped her papery wings frantically, but Lyla didn't bother to listen. She never moved from the water's edge, too intent on staring at herself in the pond.

Suddenly, before she realised what was happening, a small podgy hand had swooped down, and scooped her up, dropping her into a small, dark cell. The door was shut tight, and she was panicking.

'What on earth is happening. Where has the sun gone?' she said. She was tumbled around, turning upside down until she felt quite dizzy and sick, and the worst of it was, that every time she slipped sideways, she got prickled by a hairy caterpillar that was sharing the box with her.

Just when she thought it would never end, there was a sudden jolt, and the box was still. She was so tired now that she fell asleep, but woke with a start when a shaft of light streamed into her prison. The door had been opened just a little way!

She scrambled to her feet, and scuttled towards the opening as fast as her little spindly legs would carry her.

Before the podgy fingers could grasp hold of her again, she spread her shiny, red wings and, with a huge effort, took off like a helicopter - straight up into the air, to the complete surprise of the children.

Up, up, up she flew - into the blue sky and the racing clouds. But then, a wind blew up, and she had no idea where she was going. The old nursery rhyme kept going round and round inside her head, 'Ladybird, ladybird, fly away home - your house is on fire and your children are gone'. She was very, very frightened, and thought about how stupid she had been.

She flew and flew until she was exhausted. She flew over yellow and green fields, she flew over blue lakes and streams. She flew over villages and church steeples. She flew over farms where there were cows, pigs and horses. She flew and she flew until at last, she dropped to the ground. Surely, there was no chance she would ever see her beloved home again.

She lay there for a while, lost and confused. Then, a familiar sound brought her back to life. 'Hmmm ... hmmm ... hmmm.' It was Buzzy Bee, her friend!

She looked around again - oh yes. She had landed in one of the flowerbeds surrounding the Fairy Glen - only a wish away from her home!

Buzzy hovered over her, fussing as usual, but Lyla already felt much better for being almost home. She hitched a ride on Buzzy's back and soon, she spied her lovely familiar pond, sparkling in the sunlight through the trees.

Della was there, sitting on a water lily, preening her wings with an 'I told you so' look on her face, but Freddy just grinned a big grin, and croaked a welcoming hello.

Buzzy put Lyla down at the water's edge, and she drank and drank and drank as though she would never stop. Then, she went back home to her little house in the pine log. She heaved a sigh of relief - her children were still there, just where she had left them. A warm feeling crept over her, replacing the panic she had felt. Then, a sudden thought dawned on her, and she smiled to herself. She had not once looked at herself in the pond since she returned. She hadn't had the time!

These days, Lyla isn't so vain, although sometimes, she still catches herself gazing a bit too long into the water when she goes for a drink!

Jennifer D Wootton

Netball

Netball starts with centre,
Quickly pass the ball,
Everybody move around,
Oops it goes off court.

Quickly over here,
Let's get it up court,
Pass to me, here you go,
Yes, we've just scored.

Centre once again,
Other team defends,
'I'm free,' a teammate shouts,
The ball travels through the air.

Quickly over here,
Let's get it up court,
Pass to me, here you go,
Yes, we've just scored.

Our centre once again,
Very well caught,
Who am I going to pass to?
My friend clearly thought.

Quickly over here,
Let's get it up court,
Pass to me, here you go,
Yes, we've just scored.

Centre to the other team,
We then catch the ball,
Heading towards the goal,
We then score.

There goes the whistle,
Just been blown,
We travel off the pitch,
Happy with a 4-0 win.

Abigail Morton

Underwater Flying Lessons

When flying underwater,
Now listen, this is true.
Beware of the big fishes,
As they fly by next to you.

Flying underneath the waves,
As simple as giving cuddles.
Just as long as we remember to
Bring air tanks full of bubbles.

How do I learn? I hear your plea,
As parents say swim in the sea.

Yet what do parents know?
They've forgotten how to dream.
If they could just remember
I bet you'd hear them scream.

Now here is your first lesson.
I know it may sound daft.
But before we fly beneath the waves,
We practise in the bath.

Give us more, tell lesson two.
We want to learn, to fly like you.

To learn we must go forward.
Grab our shampoo and our soap.
Pretend you're on a pirate ship,
Hoist the main sail, pull the rope.

Our ship's come under danger
We have to walk the plank.
The treasure's been thrown overboard,
At least it's safe. It sank.

I know what you're thinking,
It's stranger than it seems.
We only fly underwater when
We do it in our dreams.

A M Williamson

Number Tree

In a corner of my garden,
I have a number tree.
A tree that blossoms in base ten
And mesmerises me.

In very early springtime
When days begin to warm,
The branches sprout with little buds
As tiny zeros form.

The buds burst into flowers
Rejoicing in the sun.
And every slender flower
Is shaped just like a one.

The petals fall in drifts of white
As tiny twos unfold.
The twos develop into threes
Which soon increase fourfold.

The fruit begins to ripen
In balmy summer air.
One day I come to see the fours
And fives hang everywhere.

Each lovely five expands in size
Then grows into a six.
The sixes swell to sevens
And soon eights enter the mix.

The eights are round and golden,
But I'm afraid to prune them.
I don't let others see the tree;
They'd shake a branch and ruin them.

So it happens every autumn
That nobody believes:
In a corner of my garden
Nines are falling with the leaves.

M W Penn

The Elves' Adventure

Winter had come to Mushroom Town; the trees had a layer of white snow making them look very pretty.

The same trees sheltered the elves' little houses in Mushroom Town so they only had a sprinkling of snow although in the nearby field it had snowed quite heavily.

All the insects had gone into hibernation, which meant they went to sleep all through winter months until the spring sunshine came again. The flowers had also gone to sleep until it was time for them to wake up in the spring sunshine.

The elves had stocked their pantries with a good supply of food, enough to see them through the long, cold winter days and nights. It was very quiet everywhere as the elves rarely came out of their snug little homes into the cold town. They spent a lot of time sat in front of their fires reading fairy stories of magic spells and adventures with witches and wizards.

As the daylight faded the elves lit tiny candles to brighten their rooms until it was time for bed. Nothing much happened in the long winter nights. Sage, the eldest elf, was sat snoozing in his rocking chair, when he recalled a story his mother had told him many years ago when he was just a little boy … This is the story Spice had told Sage as he sat on her lap, of an adventure she had as a young girl …

She had heard many tales about giant humans who came to play in the fields beyond the wood where the elves were forbidden to go. Spice decided one day to sneak out and go and see if the stories were true. She tiptoed quietly out of her house and ran down the path until on the edge of the wood she found a small gap in the bushes and settled down to watch. The giants were, of course, children but as the elves were so small they seemed like giants to Spice.

Spice watched in wonder as she saw the children making snowmen and throwing snowballs at each other, one snowball bounced off the bush where Spice was hiding causing her to pull back sharply. Spice was so fascinated that she hadn't realised that it was getting dark and the snowball had made her jump. Spice thought it was time she should slip back to her home after her adventure.

She knew she was not supposed to be there as it was a rule of Mushroom Town that no one went past the end of the wood as they could be hurt or killed if they accidentally got trodden on.

Sage thought a great deal about his mother's story and began to wonder if it was really true and if so whether the giants still went to play in the fields. He decided to go and see for himself.

Now elves have no sense of time so when Sage decided to go and have a look it did not occur to him that all the children would be grown up by now. Sage fetched out his warm coat, his long scarf and his gloves so that he would keep warm, and he set off towards the edge of the wood.

Now Sage had to pass by Dill's house on his way to the edge of the wood but did not notice that Dill had seen him go by. *I wonder where Sage is going?* Dill said to himself, I think I will follow him. So like Sage, Dill put on his warm coat and gloves and set off after him. He was surprised to see Sage suddenly disappear from view and began to run and see what had happened. To his horror he found that Sage had fallen down a hole and could not get out.

'Can you reach my hand?' Dill asked.

'I am afraid not,' replied Sage.

'Hold on,' said Dill, 'I will get some help,' and he ran back to Mushroom Town, knocking on his neighbours' doors as he went by. 'Sage is in trouble,' he cried, 'he has fallen down a hole and cannot get out, we need something to pull him out with.'

The elves decided that as they had no rope handy they would tie all their scarves together and lower that down to Sage so they could pull him out. The elves quickly made a long rope with their scarves and lowered it down to Sage who tied it around his waist and thankfully was soon back on safe land. They took Sage back to his house where he soon warmed up by his cosy fire.

'What were you doing? Where were you going?' asked Dill.

Sage sat the elves down and told them the entire story about his mother's adventure. 'I don't know if it is true or not,' said Sage, 'but I do know it is not safe to go to the edge of the wood, that is why it is forbidden.'

All the elves agreed and said they would never try to find out if the story was true as it was far too dangerous. Spice's story disappeared into elf folklore and the elves never knew or ever really cared if it was true or not.

Joan Gallen

Words

Words really annoy me sometimes,
All long and complicated.
I try to put my hands over my ears
And shout *lalalalalalala*
But that doesn't work.

Because I can still read them sometimes,
All italic and hyphenated
I try to put my hands over my eyes
And squeeze them shut
But that doesn't work.

Because then I dream sometimes
Alone and separated.
I try to avoid the words swooping down at me
So I duck and curl up so tight
But that doesn't work.

So then I write about words sometimes,
When I'm mad or frustrated.
But that makes me think about words even more -
Ahhhhhhh!
Even this hasn't worked
So I think I'll stop.

Kevin Chapman

The Sun King And The Moonraker

The croaky old frog sat down on a rock, he was exhausted after ferrying four elves from the sea on Earth all the way up to the moon. 'I need some water fast!' he croaked.

But the elves were busy exploring their new land. 'And where will we find that?' they asked anxiously, for they too were growing thirstier by the minute but all they could see was a wide expanse of dusty rock and red earth.

'Croaky' as he had become known, was secretly fed up with his four companions and wished he had never got involved with them. Elf no. 1 was too old to be truly clever, although the others thought he was. Elf no. 2 tried to be clever, but wasn't. Elf no. 3 thought he knew it all and Elf no. 4 knew a little but not much. Croaky wished he hadn't offered to follow the sun. True they had landed in water, but it was so salty they had to leave. He longed now for a nice cool place like a brook with fresh green grass and the sun king smiling benignly down on the Mother Earth.

A big, big tear welled up into his eye and dripped slowly down his green cheeks. Now here they all were, stuck on the moon's surface which was drier than a line full of washing on a hot summery day. Croaky sniffed and wondered what would become of them all.

'Can't you think of anything?' he asked Elf no. 1 crossly.

'We could go back to the sea,' suggested Elf no. 1.

Croaky was so angry he leapt high in the air with rage, 'Too salty, too salty!' he yelled from his great height. 'Oh dear, I'm right up here now and I can't get down!' he croaked. 'There is no gravity and I can't get down, oh, I'm floating away Elf 1, oh help me, do help me!'

All the elves gathered now to stand and watch in wonderment as the frog drifted up and up into space then suddenly disappeared from their sight.

Croaky felt wonderful as he drifted into a huge cloud which just happened to be filled with rain waiting to be carried down to Mother Earth. 'Bliss, bliss,' he sighed contentedly, lapping at the fresh clean rain water and wallowing his dry skin in the beautiful soft damp ball of cloud.

Elf no. 1 scratched his head, 'Mmm, what shall we do now?' he muttered to the others.

'We could try jumping like Croaky,' said Elf no. 3.

'No, no, we'd get ourselves into more trouble,' said Elf no. 2.

'Well we can't just stand here,' said Elf no. 4, 'so let's go looking for food and water.'

'Very practical,' said Elf no. 1.

Keeping very close together they all trouped off across the moon's surface to see what they could find.

'Look there!' shouted Elf no. 2, 'look, a cave!'

They all raced across towards the opening, their tiny feet and legs feeling peculiarly light and bouncy as they moved along.

Once inside the cave it was rather gloomy and dark.

'Ooh, I don't like it here,' protested Elf no. 4, 'it's far too creepy.'

'Don't be silly 4,' said no. 2, 'it's just a cave, of course it's darker, hey! I wonder what's down there.' He pointed to a passage way leading off to the left.

'Let's explore,' said no. 1. So off they went down the long, gloomy passage.

Presently they heard a strange noise coming from somewhere ahead of them. It sounded like someone taking long deep breaths of air. Just then there loomed up in front of them what appeared to be a giant elf. Dressed just like themselves in green jacket and red trousers and with a leaf-shaped hat upon his head. 'Oooh!' said Elf no. 3, 'who are you?'

The big elf-like fellow drew himself up even taller than at first as he gazed down upon the four little elves who stared up at him in great awe. 'Who am I?' he bellowed, 'why, I am the keeper of the great Moon, my name is Moonraker, but whom, may I ask are you? And how did you get here on my land?'

The jaunty four were a bit worried now, perhaps they were trespassing. They remembered on Earth that there were signs on farm gates saying 'Trespassers will be prosecuted', what if they were to be sent to prison?

Elf no. 1 showing great courage and presence of mind, squared up to the giant. 'We are lost Sir,' he said showing due deference to the giant's obvious authority.

'We didn't mean to trespass.' Then they told the giant elf how the frog had brought them here after searching for the sun king and how he had now disappeared.

The giant listened sympathetically for he could see how distressed the little elves were at being stranded on the moon. When at last they had finished telling their tale of woe, the giant let out a long, deep sigh, it was such a long, deep sigh that the blast of air rising up from his huge lungs came rushing out all at once from the large cavity of his mouth. Just like a strong wind blowing hard on a stormy day and on reaching the little group standing patiently before him, it blew them all over the cave room with such a force that they all had to hold on tight to each other in order not to be blown away altogether!

'Oooh! Please stop that Mr Moonraker,' they squealed in fright, 'or we shall all be blown away into space just like poor Croaky.'

'Stuff and nonsense,' exclaimed the giant, his whole great frame shaking with laughter now. 'What a funny little group you are, why, you are no bigger than the moonstones I rake up every day from the moon's surface. I have to keep it clear and tidy you see, in case the Earth people want to send their airships here to investigate. They must have space to land.'

The elves were very surprised to hear about this. 'Do Earth people really come here?' they asked.

'Oh yes, they like to explore you know, and sometimes meddle, Earth people can be very tiresome with their meddling into things they don't understand. They call it progress, but it takes them millions of years to do it, and then they go off to some war or other, and forget where they got to, and have to start all over again.'

The giant laughed again, shaking his huge mane of silvery hair which hung low on his shoulders and glimmered and shone as the moonbeams darted in and out of his long beard like fireflies playing through the long grass on the river banks of Earth.

'We are so thirsty and hungry Mr Moonraker, please can you help us?' cried Elf no. 3, 'could the Earth people take us back with them do you think?'

'No doubt they could,' smiled the giant, 'but would they? They don't believe in elves, and anyway they don't come here very often.'

It was all too much for Elf no. 2 and no. 4, they both began to weep. 'Then we shall never get home again!' they sobbed.

'Come, come,' said the giant elf, 'you mustn't be so pessimistic, there is always a solution to every problem. Look at me, I have been here for millions of years, but I have survived. But, if you really want to go back to that turbulent old planet Earth I will beam you down on my strongest silver beam ray, now what do you say to that?'

'Oh my dear Mr Moonraker,' exclaimed Elf no. 1, whose wrinkles were moving rapidly up and down with extreme emotion, 'would you really? How kind, we would all be most grateful to you Sir,' he paused. 'How soon may we leave?'

The giant elf sighed again. He was getting very little peace with these earthly beings, always wanting something they hadn't got, why couldn't they be content with their lot as he had been for all these years?

'Come along then, and climb up on my shoulders,' he said resignedly, and so they all swiftly clambered up his long legs until they reached his shoulders which seemed a long, long way to climb. Then they all clung tightly on as his great form lumbered its way out of the cave to the edge of the moon. There he gave a great whoosh as he shed his silvery beams of light down towards the Earth and the elves with their little legs clinging tightly astride the long beams of light found themselves hurtling through the night down towards the Earth. As they whizzed past the sun king, who was just waking up to Earth's dawn, they caught sight of the big fluffy cloud being warmed by the waking sun, and now dissolving into rain, and there was old Croaky leaping about happily 'midst the raindrops, jumping from one to another as they dripped downwards in their fall. Soon a magnificent rainbow appeared, smiling happily at the antics of the tiny earthlings in their bid to reach home.

At last they were all landed safely on the river bank, relieved and glad to be home again. How they laughed and clapped and sang. And what a feast they enjoyed as they celebrated their safe return.

What tales they would have to tell their fellow creatures. For they had all learned much from their adventures. I don't think their lives will ever be the same again, do you?

Hazel Brydon

White Rabbit

Little rabbits play in my garden and one of them is white,
To see him hopping round my lawn is quite a startling sight,
He's very shy and timid, he hasn't got a name,
He lives with all the other bunnies and isn't really tame.
If I don't see him for a while, I never think he's harmed,
I know he's always safe and sound, he has a life that's charmed,
And if you're wondering why that is, and how it is I know,
I've seen him with his little friends, the fairies love him so.

Valerie Leaver

The Freaky Clawboards

Have you ever seen the Bogeyman,
Or heard things that go bump in the night?
Because beware of the Freaky Clawboards
They can give you an almighty fright!

While it's dark, early in the morning,
Before a new day is dawning,
In the absence of the cheery sun
The nightmare has already begun!

At first the noise is faint, unclear,
And there isn't any reason to fear -
It's only the cat's claws scratching at the floor,
Then only the latch rattling on the door.
Then a large gust of wind begins to howl,
And you hear a screeching from a big barn owl.
Daddy-Long-Legs scuttles across the ceiling,
Leaving you with a creepy feeling.
The beetle and ant march for miles
Over the expanse of bathroom tiles.
The big wicker chair in the corner creaks;
A mouse in the garden shrilly shrieks.

In the stillness of the night all is a riot,
Then everything goes *deathly* quiet.

Suddenly a sound you hear
You hear it - it's coming near!

It's creaking, creeping, crawling - *close!*

Outside your bedroom door,
Creaking on your floor.

All around you - very near
The Freaky Clawboards

- Are Here!

Lauren Hesford

Forward Press Information

We hope you have enjoyed reading this book - and that you will continue to enjoy it in the coming years.

If you like reading and writing poetry drop us a line, or give us a call, and we'll send you a free information pack.

Alternatively if you would like to order further copies of this book or any of our other titles, then please give us a call or log onto our website at www.forwardpress.co.uk

Forward Press Ltd. Information
Remus House
Coltsfoot Drive
Peterborough
PE2 9JX

(01733) 898101